WALL COVERINGS
and DECORATION

WALL COVERINGS and DECORATION

Abel Banov

Jeanne Lytle

Douglas Rossig

Structures Publishing Company
Farmington, Michigan   1976

Manufactured in the United States of America

Edited by Shirley M. Horowitz

Designed by Richard Kinney

Cover photo: Hedrich Blessing Studios, Chicago.

Current Printing (last digit)
10 9 8 7 6 5 4 3 2 1

Library of Congress Cataloging in Publication Data
Banov, Abel.
    Wall coverings and decoration.

    1. Wall coverings in interior decoration.
I. Lytle, Jeanne, joint author.   II. Rossig, Douglas, joint author.   III. Title.
NK2115.5.W3B36   747'.3   76-28710
ISBN 0-912336-24-2
ISBN 0-912336-25-0 pbk.

Contents

C878615

Introduction

Centuries of civilized living have given most of us a taste for attractive surroundings. A long time has passed since the first sensitive tribesman drew pictures of deer or antelope on the crude animal skins that he had spread on the walls of his habitation to insulate him and his family from the bitter cold. We can imagine this first decorator proudly showing his handiwork to fellow tribesmen, and soon finding his companions trying to outdo him with their own drawings.

This first sensitive soul, who decorated what had been merely functional items, had to have at least a little time left over from his hunting and fishing to indulge in his decorating endeavors. Today's planning and decoration demands even more time, due to the many options and styles available.

People now have considerably more time to devote, and even those of us in modest circumstances, usually have sufficient resources for some kind of room enhancement. We have a large array of materials to beautify our wall surfaces, and we can further decorate them with art selections. We do not have to invent wall decoration; generations behind us have given us a good start. We can enjoy the fruit of this evolution from primitive decoration to today's many-faceted esthetics.

In this section, a brief history of wall coverings will be presented, and then suggestions will be made about styles on the market and how to shop for them. Information will be provided on kinds of art available for your wall treatments, other important accessories, plus wood coverings and wallboard. Also of interest and unique to this book is a chapter on the use of light in your wall scheme. In the second section you will be given techniques for putting all this together for good wall design and, in the final section, full instructions will be presented for putting up the wall coverings. The instructions are prepared by the nation's leading lecturer on wall cover application, Douglas Rossig. Although simply put, they are complete enough for the advanced training of young professional paperhangers. In fact, it is expected that this book will be used as a text at lectures for professionals.

1. Wall Covering Components

Flexible Wall Coverings— Papers, Textiles, Vinyls

BRIEF HISTORY

The Chinese invented paper around 105 A.D. It took another 600 years before paper worked its way westward

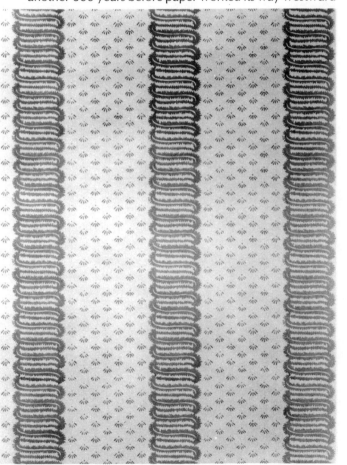

First decorated papers intended for walls were made by the **dominotiers,** *a guild of painters and papermakers. This documentary reproduction of a domino paper is by Scalamandre.*

via Arab traders, who learned the secret from captured Chinese seamen on the Indian Ocean coast. The "secret" spread to Egypt, Morocco, and Spain, finally reaching Italy, Germany and the heartland of Europe in the 11th century. But it wasn't until papermaking came to England in 1490, just a short while before Columbus blundered into the New World, that wall paper could begin development.

Fragments of the first known wallpaper were discovered at Cambridge University. Dated by scientific means, it was determined to have been made in 1509, only 19 years after paper was first made in England. Made by a printer named Hugo Goes, it was created expressly for wall decoration.

Goes then tried to imitate velvet and brocade, which already were used extensively throughout Europe to decorate walls and to keep out the cold. In this, the English and the Europeans hadn't progressed far from the primitives who had taken the same steps for insulation and comfort.

About 100 years after Goes started the wallpaper business, French makers of playing cards and small decorated sheets for book covers produced highly figured wallpapers. These producers were known as Les Dominotiers, and their work was called Domino papers, names by which succeeding imitations have also been known to this day. English papers often had embroidery designed into them, but the French were considerably more decorative in their patterns. At some time, no one knows just when, rich patrons had artists paint wallpaper for them. These painted papers have survived in a few places in England, and consist of a number of sheets butted together, each of about 30″ x 21″.

Then, in the late 1700s, the Eckhardt Brothers moved over to England from Holland and began patenting ways to silver paper so it would resemble damask and lace, which was a breakthrough because it involved more than just putting on a design; it meant having patterns with two levels of lustre, a bright surface adjoining a dull one.

At this time, making wallpaper was a slow, time-consuming process based on woodblocks, using an early form of printing known as *letterpress*. This type of printing employs a raised surface where ink is deposited prior to impression on paper.

At the turn of the 19th century, the Frenchman Louis Robert patented a machine derived from the calico cloth printing process, which had been developed 50 years earlier. Even then, it took another 40 years before a British calico printer developed a machine process that could continuously put eight colors on wallpaper. It's also significant that this process was perfected at about the same time as the development that made it possible—availability of paper in continuous lengths.

Now, mass production of wallpaper was at hand. That does not mean that hand-made products disappeared, or even declined. Fine, artistic creations continued. Such men as William Morris, a poet, book designer, political figure, and the inventor of the Morris Chair, shunned the machine. Morris was responsible for hand-printed papers which strongly influenced an entire art movement that followed closely after him, the famous Art Nouveau.

The United States was still under the influence of European taste makers, especially French. Small Domino papers, with marble-like patterns as well as others, were imported in great quantity in the 18th century. And then John Rugar of New York, John Bright of Boston, and the firm of John Howell and Son in Albany, N.Y., entered the wallpaper business. Little of their work has come down, except for wallpaper used for bandbox covers and trunk lining. Scenes were panoramic, based mainly on commemorative scenes from the American Revolution.

Quite a few wall coverings have been found in the U.S. in old mansions built in the 18th and 19th centuries. Some of them were made here, some in Europe. These have been reproduced for restoration of buildings by historical groups. Wall covering firms, usually operating under royalty agreements with the restorers, are now offering many of these patterns, although they are often only purchasable through decorators.

American wallpapers were of little interest for quite a few years. In the 1930s, with the development of silk screen printing and the influence of European art movements such as Cubism, the Bauhaus, and modernistic scenery designed for European ballet, American hand-screen firms broke away from traditional patterns and revived interest in wallpaper as an art form.

A few years ago, wallpaper manufacturers and distributors combined marketing and promotional efforts to form the Wallcovering Council. An effective staff director

was named, and succeeding directors and new association groups have advanced the cause of the industry.

As we shall see in succeeding paragraphs on how to buy wall coverings, strides have been made in removing handicaps to intelligent buying. Cooperative effort by the wall covering industry has been a help, but aggressive promotion and merchandising activity by a limited number of important producers have also been significant. Together they have stripped away the shell of conservatism that for many decades impeded acceptance of wallpaper as a primary decorating tool.

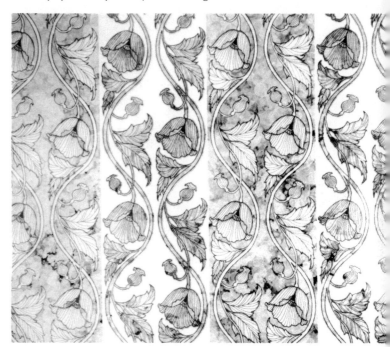

Hand-printed papers maintained high quality after mass-production methods threatened to lower it. This elegant, stylized treatment was part of the Art Deco trend in the mid-1800's (Seeman Studios photo).

Found in a restored house in Deerfield, Mass., this paper was made from linen rags and then applied with a paste so durable the paper could not be removed. Successive papers were put over it, but were removed for restoration (Scalamandre).

Buying Wall Covering

WALLCOVERING ROOM-ANALYSIS CHART

	Living	Dining	Other
alls — Dimensions			
urnishings — Style			
Main Color			
Accent Color(s)			
Upholstery — Color(s)			
Drapery — Color(s)			
Woodwork — Color			
ooring — Material			
Color(s)			
imensional Effect Wanted:			
Room (larger, smaller)			
Walls (higher, lower)			
Depth illusion			
pecial Effect Wanted:			
Room (lighter, cooler, warmer, cozier).			
Architectural interest			
Unification			

The simplest way to buy wall covering is to assign the job to a decorator and forget about it. But since a decorator's selection is usually made as part of a big and costly decorating project, not everyone will be able to do this. Before deciding to turn it all over to a decorator, read all the way through this book; you may find it's all a lot easier and more exciting than you expected.

In fact, only a small percentage of wall-covering users can afford a decorator, and an even smaller percentage of those will want to miss the opportunity to choose from and ramble among the eye-pleasing designs that literally jump from the pages of wall covering books, and from the displays in manufacturers' showrooms.

If you elect to be your own decorator, you may be overwhelmed by the wealth of patterns. Some stores boast that they have 300 to 400 books of samples. That means as many as 20,000 patterns. In addition, some stores may show as many as 1,500 display wings, some of them with two and three patterns.

When you realize that many of the patterns appearing in books and on wings are also available in color variations, you can safely figure that a wall covering shopper in a sizable decorating merchandise store has access to at least 75,000 patterns, if we count color variations (i.e., a blue, red and green plaid with a dominant red may be available with blue, or green dominant, and may also come in a set of totally different colors with their variations of dominants.)

Letting a decorator help you is one way to cope. Decorators buy from stores. They also open doors for you to showrooms that won't sell to anyone not accompanied by a decorator. These exclusive companies offer patterns, very often expensive ones, that you will see nowhere else.

But if you are going to do your own shopping, how do you avoid stupefaction when confronted by all the books and pattern wings spread before you? It's easier than it seems, once you limit your shopping to stores where knowledgeable personnel are available when you want help.

It also helps if you come prepared, after having done a modest amount of homework.

You should know these eight basics before you begin to shop for wall covering.

1. *Know* the dimensions of each wall to be decorated, and preferably, have a room diagram showing windows and doors.
2. *Know* the problems, if any, of the rooms to be decorated, such as: lots of corners; presence of high ceilings; narrow dimensions; wide dimensions; fireplace; dormers; windows; doors.
3. *Know* the type of room to be decorated (bathroom, kitchen, etc.).
4. *Know* colors of prominent decorative objects in the room, such as rugs, furniture, pictures, and sculpture.
5. *Know* dominant colors in adjoining rooms, visible from the room to be decorated.
6. *Know* the personal inclinations of those who use the room—their needs in terms of a lively or restful environment.
7. *Know* the general preference of those concerned as to pattern types.
8. *Know* the general preference, regarding wall covering material, particularly if the walls are likely to be subject to abuse.

With these "knows," a decorative consultant in the store (and many stores have certified decorators on their staff; find out which stores do) can advise you on selection.

"Know" number one is obvious: you need dimensions to determine how many rolls you require. Number two will enable the decorative adviser to recommend a pattern that counteracts your room problems. High ceilings, for example, can be counteracted with a muted or darker-toned wall covering pattern. Or, by putting the same pattern on walls and ceiling, the ceiling can appear lower. In contrast, a low ceiling will be helped by stripes or other vertical designs used on the walls in combination with a white or off-white ceiling.

The third item allows the adviser to match style with function. The fourth and fifth requirements permit harmonizing of wall colors that will be seen simultaneously. You don't want wall covering that will clash with furniture or rugs in the same room, or with visible dominant colors in other rooms.

Numbers 6, 7, and 8 are matters of courtesy, consideration, and economics. If preferences run to foils, Mylar, vinyl or hand-prints, rather than machine-printed materials, you can expect to spend more money. And you do not want to spend your money only to find that another family member particularly dislikes the type of pattern or material you have purchased.

BUYING FROM THE BOOK, AND ALTERNATIVES

Experienced shoppers know that until recently only one option, with few exceptions, was offered. You browsed through wall-covering books for patterns, ordered them, then waited a week or 10 days—if you were lucky—to receive your materials.

You can still do that, and more often than not you will only want patterns that must be ordered from a book. However, more and more stores are stocking quantities of patterns that you can pick up as you shop. You can take them home and start putting them up the same day.

These stocked patterns are usually limited in number, but the choice is widening constantly. Before you turn to books, you would do well to see if some of your needs can be filled from merchandise on hand.

Some stores, as has been true for many years, stock discontinued patterns bought from the manufacturers who closed these patterns out. These are often sold at substantial discount, and for spare rooms, work rooms, or basements, they can offer real value. Occasionally they may also be just what you want for your living room or bedroom. Just because a manufacturer discontinued a pattern does not mean it will not fill your needs or suit your tastes. Also, you may find that the pattern you order from a book is so much more expensive than the one you can get right away, that you decide to compromise on this pattern and use the savings for something else.

Some stocked items are irregulars, and should say so. If you use them you will probably have to waste some material in trimming poorly printed or damaged areas. You may waste additional material because you will probably have to cut out sections to match up adjoining strips. So buy irregulars knowing what's involved.

Items that are fresh and whole are also included in stocked merchandise. They are usually items also carried in books. The difference is that the merchant believes in their salability to such an extent that he is willing to buy them outright instead of selling them only on order. Many of them are popular items that the merchant believes he can sell fast enough to justify investing in them, in return for the better discount he will get when ordering in quantity.

In addition, some wall-covering firms are now packaging goods in plastic bags for stores that stock and are supplying special point-of-sale displays. These end displays resemble cereal displays in a supermarket, and wall covering is thus almost as easy to buy—if you let store personnel advise you.

One company now furnishes stores with a complete system including wall coverings in self-serve racks. Wall chips with samples you can take home prior to buying are offered, plus a Room Visualizer with a revolving drum

Floral designs have brightened rooms of all kinds and sizes since color was first introduced into wall coverings (photo above, Seeman; photo below, York covering courtesy of Lis King).

that holds hundreds of cards, each with a reduced photograph of a 5 foot x 5 foot section of a wall covering pattern. The patterns, as a whole, are divided into eight categories.

The shopper chooses the category that is of interest. As he or she turns a wheel on the visualizer, photographs of beautiful walls will unfold. Transparent overlays with line drawings of various rooms are used also. Any of these overlays can be picked up and placed over the pattern that pleases the customer, affording a view of a complete room setting using the chosen pattern.

Each pictured pattern on the card in the Visualizer has pertinent information as to materials in which the pattern is furnished (pre-pasted, strippable, washable, scrubbable, or stain-resistant), price, and whether it is stocked or must be ordered. It also shows how many alternate color combinations are offered in the same pattern.

Finally, the card gives the pattern number and pattern category so the customer can walk over to the proper display wing category and find a large sample of the actual pattern.

The Room Visualizer is an important advance in making the jungle of wall covering books penetrable. It will, no doubt, be adapted by other marketers.

Of necessity, the categories in the Visualizer are streamlined. They are:

1. Florals;
2. Traditionals;
3. Modern/Medallions/Tile Effects;
4. Stripes/Checks/Plaids;
5. Novelties/Special Effects/Scenics;
6. Textures/Mini Prints;
7. Trellis/Grilles;
8. Children's.

The broad list of patterns offered by the industry are fully encompassed by the eight categories. But for purposes of pattern categories, and following considerable study and discussions with persons long experienced in the industry, another pattern grouping is presented here. Hopefully, it may give the shopper more leeway in identifying the type of pattern in mind. The categories are:

1. Florals;
2. Period (including Colonials and Provincials, which are identified as Traditional);
3. Modern Medallion and Simulated Ceramics;
4. Geometric (Multi-linear, Stripes, Checks, Plaids);
5. Antique Textile (Damask and Paisley);
6. Conversation Pieces (Novelties, Special Effects, and Scenics);
7. Textures (Three-dimensionals, including flocks, grass cloths, burlaps, and Shiki silks);
8. Trellis and Grilles;
9. Children's.

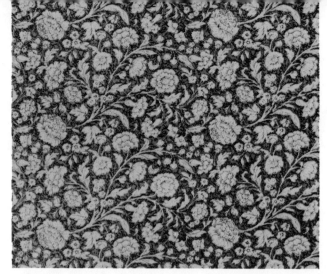

Although wall covering as we know it was not used in the Renaissance period, the finely drawn flowers in this tone-on-tone embossed design are typical of modern patterns derived from classic textiles produced in 15th and 16th century Italy.

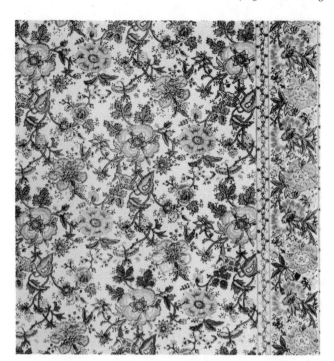

Finely detailed designs inspired by country artisans characterize French Provincial wall coverings (Seeman Studios photo).

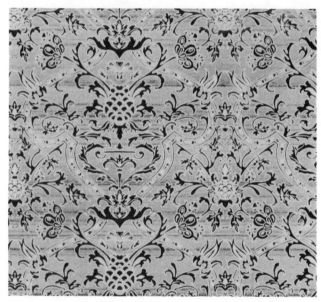

Embellishment added to earlier classical balance characterizes Baroque design. This French brocade is on a ground of ultra-modern Mylar polyester film (Seeman Studios photo).

The Rococo Period broke away from the old balance in classical design. Shown here is Chinoiserie, or the Chinese-style. Other important Rococo hallmarks are scallop shells and rocks as well as flowers, leaves, and bamboo shoots (Seeman Studios photo).

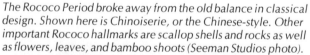

Pattern found in a restoration at Ambridge, Penn., illustrates symmetry and graceful lines found in the Louis XVI Period (Scalamandre).

13

Impressive Georgian homes used formal, low-keyed wall decorations, many of them with stripes. Scenics were also found. This paper was found in a restored home in Old Deerfield, Mass. (Photo on right, Lis King; photo above, Scalamandre).

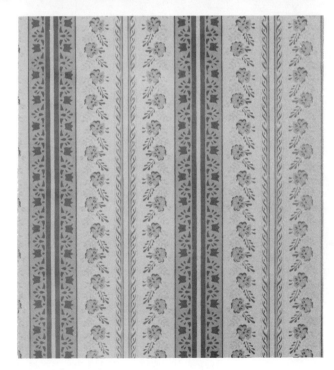

PATTERN CLASSES

Florals

Since real flowers are universally favored for room decorations because of their association with fresh air and sunshine, it is not surprising that florals, including chintz, are the most popular wall covering pattern.

Floral patterns are available for any purpose: small designs to make a small room look large, and large patterns with dark, strong colors to make a large room seem smaller. Because they are so popular, florals cross over into other categories. You will find florals printed on textures and impressed on trellises, grilles and geometrics.

Florals have been popular ever since color was added to wallpaper. Many flowery designs from the 18th century fit into today's decor, and at least one European firm specializes in old floral designs.

High-quality florals by artistic designers may be bought at high prices, and mass-produced florals abound at low prices. Skill in handling color marks the difference.

Period (Including Traditional)

This classification includes the category usually described in the industry as Traditional, which embraces only Colonial and Provincial patterns. We believe the consumer desiring a selection linked to historical periods would be better served if we introduce a broader category that goes beyond Colonial and Provincial patterns and add pattern groups that have never been classified. We will call the entire group *Period*. In this way, we can consider the historical eras that yielded significant styles.

Accordingly, we will give brief descriptions of Renaissance; baroque; rococo; Louis XVI; Directoire; Regency; Empire; Restoration; and Colonial and Provincial.

Renaissance. Renaissance patterns combine realism and accuracy, good form and pictorial balance. The Renaissance, as the name implies, brought a rebirth of classical forms in sculpture, which was noticeable also in painting and in the minor arts such as glass decoration and woodwork.

Baroque. The era that marked a reaction to the cold formalism of the Renaissance brought a freedom, and often an excess, of design. The movement started in Italy in the late 1500s and spread to France in the era of Louis XIII, reaching its peak in Louis XIV's reign. Baroque decoration is characterized by extravagance, grandiosity and richness. It came in a period of great prosperity, the crest of French grandeur. It is found in much of the Louis XIV French architecture.

Rococo. Early in the 18th century in France, Louis XV ascended the throne. In reaction to the rather heavy decorative style of the final stages of the baroque period, lightness of style developed, characterized at first by

designs with rocks (rocaille) and scallop shells (coquille), hence the name "rococo." This period marks the onset in France of Romanticism, which began a return to nature and a departure from the weighty, balanced forms in architecture and art that were found in classicism.

In rococo decor, flowers, leaves, stems, and bamboo shoots are prominent. Because during this period the French became enamored of Chinese decor, an entire branch of rococo design was derived from the Chinese. It is called Chinoiserie.

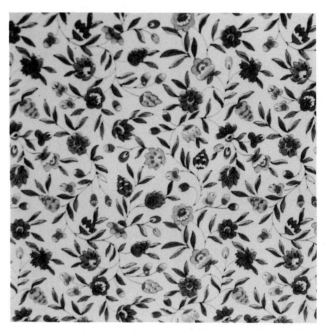

Sumptuous styles went out with Louis XVI, and simple printed cottons and chintz followed and influenced wall decor of this period as seen in this Directoire pattern (Lenox Chintz).

Textile patterns were used in the reign of Napoleon I, as well as scenes of the Emperor's exploits (Lenox Damask).

MATCHING WALL COVERINGS
TO YOUR ROOM'S PERIOD DECOR

Period	Main Characteristics of Wall Decor
Baroque	Historical or mythological scenes; rich brocades, velvets and damasks; carved ornate molding on walls and paintings; medallions.
Rococo (Louis XV)	Chinese motifs; monkey motifs; printed cottons; shepherdess' hat; basket and crook; bagpipe, horn and tambourine; bouquets and garlands of roses, daisies, etc.; Cupid motif; English flocks, and Toiles de Jouy.
Louix XVI (Neoclassic)	Rectangular panels; semi-circles, segments and ellipse used; stretched textiles; scenic papers; simulated bas relief sculpture of classical figures; ornaments where garlands, festoons, wreaths of roses, daisies and chrysanthemums are commonly tied by a ribbon in a bow knot whose ends float; Pompeiian arabesques and leaves arranged in scrolls; Greek ornaments—honeysuckle motif, carved figures with twisted bands of strings; cherubs; Cupid's bow and darts; scenes from La Fontaine's Fables; shepherds; farm tools; wheat sheaves; beribboned rustic hats; nude and draped mythological figures; sphinxes; vases; and masks; ascending balloons.
Directoire	Resembles Louis XVI, with addition of spears; drums; Liberty Cap; plough; flail; scythe; and sheaves of wheat; striped patterns; draped and plaited textiles hung below draped wall valance extending around the room.
Empire	Pompeiian inspiration—columns and pilasters; classical motifs; marbelized effects; stretched, shirred, or loosely draped textiles; sphinx with upraised wings; winged lions and disks; vultures; cobras; obelisks and hieroglyphs from Egypt; classic forms—amphora, arabesques; honeysuckle, winged victories; dancing girls; sacrificial scenes; rams; horse's heads; swans; swords. Much flock imitating damask and velvet and plaited textiles; vignetted groups of Empire figures in gardens; striped patterns; Napoleon victories; diamond borders around medallions.

American Periods

Period	Main Characteristics of Wall Decor
Early American (1608-1720)	Prewallpaper era; whitewash, usually Spanish brown, somewhat like brick; also azure blue; grayed blue; yellow; and olive-green.
Colonial, or Georgian (1720-1790)	First wallpaper imported 1737; scenics; all-over patterns; Chinese patterns; damask, chintz, or other textiles; walls with painted (often painted mustard, off white, brown, olive, or deep red with brownish cast) and unpainted woodwork.

Period	Main Characteristics of Wall Decor
Federal, or Post-Colonial (1790-1820)	Same as Directoire in France.
Greek Revival (1820-1860)	Same as Empire in France.
Victorian (1840-1880)	Big floral patterns; lots of gilt; busy patterns with line borders dividing scenes; owls and animals; imitations of William Morris' flowers, tiles and trellises with birds, boughs and fruit, with their near two-dimensional work, were best; mica used for brilliance, anticipated foil.

Louis XVI. If the Rococo period in France brought delicate natural objects to the forefront, they were soon carried to excess. To counter the excess, designers in the period identified with the reign of Louis XVI began to feature restrained patterns. Straight lines and symmetry took over, with proportions made slender and colors grayed and lightened. A happy blend of classicism and romanticism was achieved.

Colonial and Provincial. In the late 18th century, native arts and crafts played a part in the decor of homes where the crafts were developed. Those designs derived from the American colonies are called *Colonial;* those derived from the provinces of France are called *French Provincial.*

Georgian. In the reigns of various Georges (George I, II, III), a return to Renaissance styles took place. In this era of the Industrial Revolution great wealth was acquired. Formal, not-too-showy but nevertheless impressive homes, many with their famous Sheraton, Hepplewhite, and Chippendale furniture, were constructed. Wall covering design was balanced and elegant—large scenes of the countryside in the classic style were popular, as were flowers lovingly portrayed, emerging from urns. Often, designs were marked off with striped borders.

In the Georgian period, the character of what was to become the United States was forming, and so were the tastes of influential colonists. Mount Vernon, our national shrine, is Georgian; Monticello is done in American Classic, a Georgian derivative.

Directoire. When the French Revolution led to the elevation of a five-man executive known as the Directory, styles in dress and in interior decoration changed, and the restrained sumptuousness of the Louis XVI period was succeeded by an outright return to classicism. Because agriculture was glorified, ploughs, scythes, and wheat were featured. Inlaid wood on walls and furniture was replaced by painted and waxed wood. Rich fabrics disappeared and printed cottons and chintzes took their place. Wallpapers were plain and striped, and many walls in homes that would otherwise have been richly decorated had only tinted paint.

English Regency. The French Directoire period influenced British styles in the 10 years of regent rule, made necessary by the insanity of George III (the ruler at the time of the American Revolution).

Styles were simplified. The English turned to Greek classical forms; instead of agricultural objects, the honeysuckle was glorified.

Empire. Wallpapers became very popular in France during the period of Napoleon I. Lower costs, for one thing, helped increase the public's interest; the cylinder press had reduced prices. Patterns were derived from textiles, which meant that velvets and damasks were imitated. Patterns featured draped and plaited textiles; others showed vignettes of groups of costumed Empire figures lolling about in gardens. Like all art of the period, wallpapers also portrayed Greek and Roman architecture and landscapes, and Napoleonic events.

Modern Medallion and Simulated Ceramics

These patterns are characterized by confinement of the pattern within an outline. Medallions confined within outlines may be oval, rectangular, or round. Simulated ceramics are confined within the outlines of whatever is simulated, as, for example, tile.

Geometric

Lines and curves are combined into eye-catching designs that blend in with many room arrangements. Rooms with modern furniture are often decorated with large, bold geometric figures, sometimes on a foil ground. Checks, polka dots, and plaids are also offered.

Antique Textile

Textile motifs borrowed from antique cloths have become popular through the years in wall covering.

Damasks. Cloth-derived damask wall covering features highly stylized florals and foliage combined with architectural and other details. Damasks are designed to have two levels of light reflection, strengthening the texturing. Some damasks are flocked to give the feel of a third dimension.

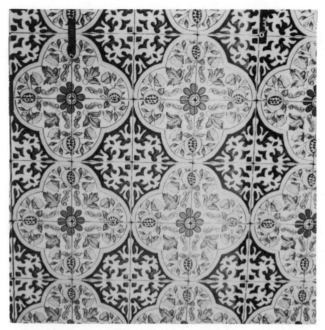

Simulated ceramics may use brick or tile as sources. Some are embossed and actually reproduce a third dimension, as does this Spanish tile (Walltex tile).

Modern furniture is often set off by a strong geometric pattern (Lenox Geometric).

17

English toiles have cheerful birds and butterflies, accented by thistles and ferns. This is an example of one pattern available only to decorators (English Toile, Brunschwig). Other patterns (photo below) tell a story.

Old-town motif for a nostalgic wall (Walltex).

Vintage ads are eye-compelling and make an interesting conversation piece. They are played well against a plaid wall (Lis King photo).

Summer scene gives feeling of movement to a potentially spare, static room (Lis King photo).

Paisley. Exotic wall coverings derived from fine woolen shawls originally made in Kashmir, India, have been offered in a wide variety. They are the *Paisleys,* with graceful, balanced designs combining detailed components ranging from small leaves to exotic crowns and royal vestments. In the proper room setting, they create an air of mystery and adventure.

Toiles. A range of rural scenes and classical allegories printed in a single color, usually blue, brown, or red, are known as Toiles because they are derived from fabrics printed and made at Jouy, France, between 1766 and 1811, and known as toiles de Jouy. Mostly landscapes and figures, they could be considered scenics.

Conversation Pieces

Wall-covering designs intended to call attention to themselves, rather than just decorate, are included in this category. They include Novelties, Special Effects, and Scenics.

Novelties. Just about any pattern that doesn't fit into any of our other categories could be called a novelty. However, the designation is reserved for patterns that usually portray figures in the midst of some sort of action. This could be children romping in the woods, or a mother carrying a babe in arms and with a tot trailing along, or it could be an old-fashioned street scene with barber shop, saloon, drug store, and cracker-barrel grocery; or it could be a scene at an old-time baseball game, complete with red flannel undershirts peeping out of short sleeves.

Special Effects. An illusion on a wall achieved by a wall covering is called a Special Effect. To achieve this, for example, you can put up a woodland scene into which it seems you could step—put on a wall, even on doors, so that the illusion would only be broken when the door is opened.

Scenics. For the homeowner who wants his art as part of the wall rather than hanging from it, scenics are offered. These are virtually wide, panoramic pictures that when skillfully put together on the wall are presentable. Some hand-screened scenics show skylines of cities, woodlands, and even scenes from famous operas—to mention only a few subject classes.

Textures

Three-dimensional effects that aim at the texture and feel of cloth, velvet, grass, silk, and other materials are accomplished with the use of synthetics. Other textures are from natural materials, such as honeysuckle vines from the Orient that are marketed as grass cloths; burlap from the East, and oriental silks. The most common textures are flocks, made by depositing finely ground particles on an adhesive until a gentle profile appears.

The impression and the color of nature, with all the brightness and movement of today's materials (photo below, Katzenbach and Warren; above, Walltex).

Three-dimensional, embossed designs look and feel like woven goods, velvet, or silk. Some, such as grass cloth and Shiki silk, are the real thing (Lenox—Texture in weave).

(Above) This fantasy design can make a smaller wall seem larger (Lis King photo).

(Right) A basic trellis like this one is often embellished with vines or flowers (Walltex).

Trellis and Grilles

These could be classified with Geometrics, since they consist of lines, but they are shapes of common objects rather than of abstract forms. Moreover, they are embellished with vines or flowers, or whatever suits the fancy of the designer.

Children's

For children's rooms you can choose from a broad class of patterns, all with a distinctive juvenile appeal— animals, clowns, letters of the alphabet, numbers, or anything likely to appeal to a child's fancy.

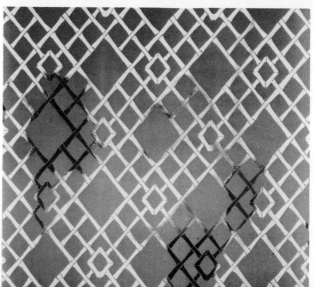

(Bottom right) Grilles add spaciousness to a room by carrying the eye across in one continuous sweep. This one has a Mylar polyester ground, and sparkles (Seeman Studios photo).

Characteristics
of Materials

For a decorative item such as wall covering, the consumer can be expected to be highly pattern-conscious. On the other hand, the material bearing the pattern should not be treated lightly.

The choice of paper vs. vinyl can mean the difference of several years' wear. And if you decide on a tough vinyl wall covering, the kind of backing you select will determine removability when you decide you want a fresh look on the walls.

The method of printing matters, too. A machine-printed wall covering will not have the lively quality found in the hand-screened product.

You will find that the more interesting materials such as foil, Mylar, grass cloth, and textiles are more difficult to put up than paper and vinyls, but they extend enormously your range of patterns and effects.

In the next few pages we will describe briefly the various materials used for wall covering and will show in charts their advantages and disadvantages. For detailed instructions on applying all the various materials, see Section 3. Here are the materials.

WALLPAPER

Wallpaper is the most common of the wall coverings, and the oldest, with the exception of textiles that were made for other purposes several centuries ago but were also applied for wall decor. Wallpaper comes in two basic types—those printed by machine, and those printed by hand.

Machine-printed Wallpapers

Mass-produced, lower priced wall coverings are printed in large quantities on roller presses. Their one big disadvantage, in addition to lower quality in design, is difficulty of removal. The exception here is the strippable type. The four types are *untrimmed, pre-trimmed, pre-trimmed* and *pasted,* and *strippable.* (See Chart 1 for advantages and disadvantages of each type.)

1. MACHINE PRINTED WALLPAPERS

Type	Advantages	Disadvantages	Adhesive Used
Untrimmed	Low cost; quick preparation; can be applied after pasting; uniform rolls.	Needs to be trimmed; hard to remove.	Any inexpensive paste
Pre-trimmed	No need to trim unless out of line; uniform rolls in matching & shading.	Edges often out of line; sheet may dry out at edges after pasting; hard to remove; limited quality in patterns.	Any inexpensive paste
Pre-trimmed & Pre-pasted	Eliminates pasting; good on porous and semi-porous walls and on unsealed old wallpaper.	Limited quality of patterns; excessive paste buildup on smooth, hard surfaces requires special care; hard to remove.	None
Strippable	Easy to repair; tear-resistant; easy to apply.	Stiff; no stretching; hard to butt on irregular surfaces; limited quality in patterns.	Wheat paste, if any

A patchwork design such as this could have been done by a machine, but hand-screening gives better colors and enables almost endless color combinations (Lis King photo).

Hand-printed Wallpapers

For those who don't mind spending considerable money for the finer things in life, hand-printed wallpapers offer a rich hand-painted effect. While found in retail stores in considerable number, some of the more elegant designs are sold only through decorators and at special showrooms in major cities.

Considerable flexibility in color combinations are offered by some of the smaller and medium-sized hand-printed wall covering firms. Customers can spot a design they like in one set of colors, and the store operator or show room manager can arrange to have it done in the desired color combination.

Hand-printing is another name for silk screen art produced in a semi-automatic process. Colors are closely related to paint used by artists for fine art; in this, hand-printing differs markedly from machine-printing, which only uses colored inks.

In the process, the designer puts his art on a clear plastic sheet. Through this sheet, the design is flashed on a photo-sensitized silk screen which is developed, leaving clear the areas where color will be added to the paper and blotting out the area that will be free of color. The screen is fixed by a hinge to a table so it can be lifted up to receive the sheets of paper and then lowered onto the paper while an operator spreads paint over the screen to work it through the tiny openings in the screen mesh and so onto the paper to make the design. A screen is made for each color.

Hand-Print Flocks. To make hand-printed flock papers with a velvet-like touch, the same silk-screen technique is used but colored adhesive is transferred to paper instead of paint. After the design is transferred in adhesive, the paper is advanced to a flocking device, which floods it with a transparent plastic dust, colored as closely as possible to the color of the adhesive constituting the design.

Since the adhesive can be tinted to the exact color desired, the limiting factor in achieving what is specified is the color of the flock. Since a fairly good selection of flock colors is offered, and since variations are lessened because of the transparency of the flock, flocked hand-prints offer considerable creative breadth to a decorator.

Textured Surface. Cork dust is laid in heavy, somewhat embossed patterns on white paper and then hand-printed to give textured effects. Fairly uniform

2. HAND-PRINTED WALLPAPERS

Type	Advantages	Disadvantages	Adhesive Used
Flat Paper Stock	Short soaking period; hides seams more easily; clear protective films usually on face; rich-looking; wide selections of patterns.	Wrinkling problem when heavy oil inks are used; seams look shiny with hard rolling.	Wheat paste
Glossy Stock	Same as above.	Curls at seams when pasted; poor resistance to water; stains if paste not removed immediately; undersurface blemishes show up clearly; lining paper usually needed.	Wheat paste
Flock Surface	Rich, velvety appearance.	Problem joining at seams; care needed to avoid paste damage at seams; lining paper needed; seams may curl; surface clean-up is difficult; annoying falloff of flock.	Wheat paste
Textured Surface	Easy to hang; seams hold well on lined wall; can be repainted.	Stiff; often cracks; usually needs lining paper.	Wheat paste

coloring has improved these materials over their original form, which left much to be desired in color matching between rolls and sometimes even in the same roll. Cork is also used in thin wafers on colored paper, usually black, orange, or red. The texture over the colored ground is attractive. Known as Spanish or Portuguese cork paper, it is often selected where a warm, Mediterranean look is wanted. (See Chart 2 for advantages and disadvantages of each type of hand-printed wallpaper.)

VINYLS

Vinyl wall covering is made of vinyl chloride sheet, a strong, easy-to-handle material. Vinyls have been growing in popularity to such an extent that they are probably approaching paper in volume of use. Like paper, vinyl wall covering may be machine printed or hand-printed.

Machine-Printed

In general, machine-printed vinyls are more costly than their paper counterparts. They offer one big advantage: they are readily removed from the wall by separating the vinyl layer from its paper backing and pulling it off. The paper remains as a base for the next wall covering, with the aid of sizing.

Another advantage is washability. Most are also pre-trimmed, which saves some bother in application.

Hand-Printed

Most of these come with paper backing, mainly because experience has proven that better printing results when paper is used.

Selvage or a waste-edge is always found on these because the hand-screening process requires edges for handling, and no method has yet been devised for removing these mechanically without interfering with ability of the applicator to match strips. These heavy vinyls are printed in the same manner as hand-printed paper.

Cloth-Backed Vinyls

Various cloths, canvas, and gauze are used for vinyl backing. The vinyl itself comes in gauges ranging from thin to thick, and some are almost board-like.

A wide variety of textured effects are worked into cloth-backed vinyls, many of them effective simulations of silk, moire, velvet, and wood. Because of the cloth backing they are relatively easy to hang and very easy to strip off the wall. (See Chart 3 for advantages and disadvantages of vinyl wall covering.)

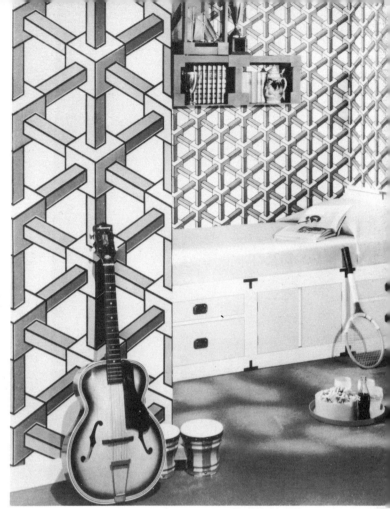

Bold designs, not needing subtle colors, use machine printing on vinyl. For a teenager's room, vinyl's cleanability and easy removal are important.

Where moisture and scrubbing are likely to be frequent, a tough fabric-backed vinyl sacrifices nothing in the way of style and beauty (Lis King photo).

FOILS

Instead of paper or vinyl plastic sheet, some wall covering, even flocked, is printed on aluminum foil with either a paper or cloth backing. Foils are moderately expensive, but they have an elegance that justifies it. A metallized Mylar gives some of the effects of foil, but has a softer quality. (See Chart 4 for advantages and disadvantages of foil wall coverings.)

This sleek, light-reflective paper combines the advantages of foil highlights and vinyl durability (from Fashion Originals Collection by General Tire, photo courtesy of Lis King).

3. VINYL WALL COVERING

Type	Advantages	Disadvantages	Adhesive Used
Paper Backed	Machine-printed versions are usually pre-trimmed; many are thin and pliable; washable; easy to remove; printing is usually superior to cloth-backed.	Nonbreathing may lead to mildew; hand-printed versions need trimming; have persistent odor; heavy versions are hard to adjust on wall.	Vinyl
Cloth Backed	Easy to hang and butt; very easy to remove; hard to tear; easy to patch; seams bond well; can be painted over.	They shrink; seams pull apart with incorrect use of wheat paste; nonbreathing, may lead to mildew.	Part powdered vinyl, part pre-mixed

4. FOIL WALL COVERING

Type	Advantages	Disadvantages	Adhesive Used
Paper Backed	Elegant appearance.	Expensive; needs trimming; needs lining paper; not stretchable for seaming; tight butt is difficult; special trimming steps needed; paper backing swells with moisture.	Part pre-mixed vinyl and powdered vinyl
Cloth backed	Elegant appearance; pre-trimmed; no lining paper needed.	Expensive, can't be stretched in seaming.	Vinyl; Wheat paste

BURLAP

Ordinary jute and hemp sack cloth, used for ages as packing, has in recent years been adopted for an effective burlap wall covering.

Some burlaps come plain. Others are hand-printed very effectively; in fact, the slightly fuzzy print effect adds to its charm.

Burlaps are sometimes laminated to a vinyl facing to make them washable and resistant to abuse for institutional and industrial use. Most burlaps are not to be washed. The burlap surface is such that it hardly shows dirt.

Most burlaps sold today have paper backing, which is necessary to stabilize the meshing of the threads and to permit satisfactory pasting and seam-butting. (See Chart 5 for advantages and disadvantages of burlap wall covering.)

FELT

Some people find felt, particularly green, a relaxing material to have around. Because it is soft, it is used where sound absorption is sought. Difficult to hang, it should preferably be handled by professionals. (See Chart 6 for advantages and disadvantages of felt wall covering.)

Imported burlap with paper backing to stabilize the natural fibre was introduced after World War II (Lenox Burlap).

5. BURLAP WALL COVERING

Type	Advantages	Disadvantages	Adhesive Used
Paper backed	Stabilized weaves; dirt doesn't show.	Not washable; large rolls; strips must be checked for off-shades; lining paper usually needed; adhesive moisture must be controlled.	Wheat paste or cellulose
Unbacked	——	Not washable; shrinks. Use lining paper.	Same as above
Vinylized	Washable; durable	Vinyl coat may separate if burlap gets wet in application period; lining paper often needed.	Pre-mixed vinyl

6. FELT WALL COVERING

Type	Advantages	Disadvantages	Adhesive Used
Paper backed	Fine appearance; sound-absorbing.	Very difficult to hang without adhesive staining; shrinks; needs lining paper for best results.	Powdered vinyl
Unbacked	Good appearance; sound-absorbing.	Very difficult to hang without adhesive staining; wide versions require two persons to hang; shrinks; needs lining paper.	Pre-mixed vinyl

Natural grass cloth, actually made from honeysuckle vine, brings natural beauty to your rooms.

This delightful oriental wall covering is misnamed. It should be called honeysuckle cloth, because it is made from vine of that species. Sun-dried and pulped, it is then made into the fiber that is woven into the ''grass'' cloth.

Grass cloth is backed with paper and is far from easy to apply. Nor are shading and coloring uniform. With natural grass cloth, some users go to great lengths to select strips that come close to matching each other. Still other users prefer to let nature take its course, and use the strips as they come.

For uniform grass cloth, synthetic versions are now offered. These are made of cellulose fibers, and color and texture are the same throughout most production runs; but then, you don't have the fresh look of nature. An interesting variant of grass cloth has a foil backing, which gives a subdued metallic background to both the natural textured product and the synthetic. (See Chart 7 for advantages and disadvantages of grass cloth wall coverings.)

TEXTILES

Among the most beautiful and most expensive wall coverings available to the decorator are various textiles that are either suitably prepared for immediate use or may be used, with considerable care, after purchase from a yard-goods dealer.

These include natural silks, hand-printed silk, oriental linen, cork-textured fabric, paperbacked fabric—among those specially targeted for wall covering users—and ordinary fabric or upholstery fabric without backing that may be bought to match a pattern already in a room.

Natural Silk

Natural silk, known as Shiki silk, has inconsistent shading, just like grass cloth, and the color bands are more evident because the texturing is so delicate.

Hand-Printed Silk

Hand-printed silks, very costly, contain designs aimed at utilizing the unique texture of silk. More often than not, the designs are oriental.

Backed Oriental Linen

These come in various colors and, in some instances, hand printing is used to take advantage of the texture.

Paper-Backed Fabric

Numerous wall covering firms now offer matching fabrics for walls, drapes or furniture. Fabric for the walls is laminated to paper to facilitate application. To permit cleanup, a sheet of vinyl is sometimes laminated to the face.

The patterns available are numerous.

7. GRASS CLOTH

Type	Advantages	Disadvantages	Adhesive Used
Japanese Natural	Natural beauty; stretches lengthwise.	If soaked too long grass separates from backing; often needs lining paper; no width-wise stretch; cuts with effort; butting is difficult.	Wheat paste
Synthetic	Expands when wet; stretches lengthwise.	Must be hung immediately after pasting; seams of heavy versions are hard to butt; frequent unevenness of edges; won't stretch widthwise.	Wheat paste
Foil-backed	Adds to appearance.	More costly; foil prevents stretching on application, so it's more difficult to apply.	

Unbacked Fabric

The sky is the limit on the use of unbacked fabric if the person applying it avoids staining with paste. A somewhat stretched look is characteristic, and may not please some persons.

Upholstery Fabric

Because upholstery is usually heavy, difficulty in cutting these fabrics is often experienced. When embossing extends to the back, heavy adhesive is required to get a dependable bond to the wall. (See Chart 8 for advantages and disadvantages of textile wall coverings.)

Soft, Embossed Surfaces

Deeply embossed vinyl-fabrics backed with polyurethane foam to provide strength are used for unusual decorative effects. They also yield extras in the form of sound absorption and cushioning where youngsters are prone to collide with walls.

The tufted quilt-like materials come in a range of colors (various shades of gold, blue, green, brown, and black and white) and can be tacked down like upholstery or applied with almost any adhesive, since the backing is porous.

Application is simple. Clean surface, after cutting material needed with a scissors. No patching or repairing of original surface is needed, since the thick material completely covers it.

Colamco, Inc., which makes deeply tufted covering, also offers decorative panels in similar materials as accents for rooms. These mural panels, like the yard goods, are easily cleaned with warm water and a mild detergent.

8. TEXTILE WALL COVERINGS

Type	Advantages	Disadvantages	Adhesive Used
Hand printed Silk	Design, added to beauty of silk; screening ink helps bind backing.	Extra care needed in butting edges; edges not always accurately aligned.	Cellulose
Backed Oriental Linen	Soft, easy to work with, stretches moderately, both directions.	Usually highly porous; care needed to avoid excess wetting of face.	Pre-sized wheat paste
Paper-backed Fabric	No seeping of paste; reduces edge-raveling; no stretched appearance.	Occasionally patterns are out of line; lining paper usually needed.	Powdered vinyl
Unbacked Fabric	Allows matching other textiles in room.	Paste may stain face; extreme care needed in hanging to avoid stretched look, wrinkles and creases.	Powdered vinyl with less than usual water.
Upholstery Fabric	Very durable; permits matching furniture upholstery.	Requires heavy cutting; may have embossed back, requiring extra heavy adhesive use.	Pre-mixed vinyl
Silk, plain (Shiki Silk)	Striking beauty.	Inconsistent shading and color; special, difficult hanging methods; very costly; curling ends make pasting difficult; lining paper needed; excessive wetting separates paper backing.	Cellulose

Wall Accessories

Walls are the backdrop for decorative schemes—areas that can be broken up by harmonious but symmetrically arranged groupings. Thus pictures and other decorative accessories can be considered tools for harmony and symmetry. The colors must harmonize, and their placement must accent, but not conflict with, the room's wall covering, symmetry, and architectural design.

Guides for harmonious and symmetrical room decoration come in Section 2. This chapter will just discuss the accessories.

Types of art for wall decoration, along with three-dimensional wall decorations such as veneers, mirror tiles, plaques, bird-like figures, sconces, and clocks are described. Other coverings that can be adhered or hung will also be included. Whatever must be nailed down, such as paneling, will be covered in a later chapter.

ART

Art objects can be obtained at varying degrees of cost, usually proportional to the rarity of the object and/or the reputation of the artist and his own opinion of his work, founded usually on the prices that other patrons have been willing to pay. Established standards for pric-even then usually less valuable than oils of comparable size by the same artist. Such works of art, like oils, are one of a kind. A fine work in watercolor or pastel, which is a kind of colored chalk demanding considerable skill, is to be preferred to a poor work in oil.

To the one-of-a-kind oils, watercolors, and pastels (and gouaches, temperas, and a few other one-of-a-kind materials named according to the material used), we can add works of art that can be obtained in multiple copies.

The most desirable of these are usually original prints, which means they come from a design that was created especially for this multiple production; the next desirable are photo-mechanically reproduced prints.

Original prints and the most desirable of the photo-mechanically reproduced prints are made in limited numbers. The mechanically reproduced prints that are published without a limit on their number are, as a rule, inferior to original prints and limited-edition mechanically reproduced prints. Under mechanically reproduced prints, in addition to those printed by presses, we include photographs because they require machines for their production and because fine art photographs are frequently issued in limited editions.

Oils

These are most frequently painted on canvas but board or plywood, and occasionally paper, can also be used.

The coloring substance, as the name indicates, is based on one or several oils, usually linseed oil, but nowadays safflower oil is also used. Colors are derived from various pigments. Some of them are natural colors such as red and brown clays, others are synthetic colors such as the organic colorfast pigment used in paint for automobiles, refrigerators and other items where color must last a long time.

Inferior paintings are often made from inferior materials that will crack up in a short while. The unwary buyer may pay high prices for art that is poor both in spirit and in physical makeup.

Because the finished products resemble those in oil, we will also consider acrylic painting. They are based on acrylic resins, a synthetic material related to Plexiglass and Lucite. These water-thinnable resins (oils are thinned with turpentine or mineral spirits) are made in various grades.

Artist Value. What you will have to pay for the oil that pleases you, no matter where you find it, will depend on the reputation of the artist and his own opinion of his work, founded usually on the prices that other patrons have been willing to pay. Established standards for pricing good art do not exist. Reputation and the ability of an artist to hold out for a price determine what you pay.

In the event that you don't know enough artists to provide you with a broad selection, consult reputable art galleries. Remember this about buying from a gallery: there are lots of phony sellers. The most legitimate believe sufficiently in the work of the artists they handle to either buy works outright or to handle them strictly on a commission basis. Others are semi-vanity galleries, which charge the artist for the "privilege" of hanging in the gallery. Their clients are usually artists who may not be good enough to get a real gallery.

Oil paintings rank highest among two-dimensional art forms due to their range and permanence (Joan H. Banov, N.Y.).

Watercolors

The medium used for watercolors is water-thinnable. Colors are transparent. Because the materials are water-sensitive and cannot be worked over, the artist must work unerringly.

Fine watercolor artists show a level of skill perhaps as great, and sometimes greater, than the skill of those working in oils. Nonetheless, watercolors are not as highly regarded as oils. One clearcut reason is the perishable nature of watercolors. They're on paper, and if water gets to them, they are spoiled. Not so with oils. Watercolors also require protection by glass, plus additional care in handling and cleaning. Clear plastic replacements for glass have recently removed this disadvantage.

Watercolors, like oils, are sold at both galleries and "schlock" art stores. Care must be exercised when shopping for them, just as with oils.

Pastels

Pastels created by serious artists have a freshness that results from the freedom with which the artist can work. Each stroke of the colored chalk-like stick must be done accurately but it need not be dipped periodically, as must a brush, into a palette-borne color pot. The creative wellspring is allowed to flow undiminished, and the sprightliness and clarity of the work virtually shine out.

Like watercolors, pastels must be framed behind glass, or clear plastic sheets, and they share with watercolors the possibility of easy damage from broken glass or moisture.

Because pastels do not enjoy the popularity of oils or watercolors, very fine work—equivalent to or often superior to many oils and watercolors when by fine artists—can often be purchased at low cost.

Pastels, like watercolors, have been painted by some of the world's great artists. Many of the inspired French impressionists and numerous modern masters, including Picasso, Chagall, and Braque, have worked effectively with them.

Drawings

Work done with pen and ink, pencil or charcoal-sticks is referred to as a drawing. Drawings are perhaps the freest, most spontaneous of all the forms of art, because the artist has direct access to his medium. He doesn't need to dip a brush, work with acid, or even to worry about flaking of his pastel-stick. The only restraint he has is the sharpness of his pen, pencil, or charcoal stick.

Like pastels, watercolors, and prints, drawings are usually protected by a glass or plastic sheet and are normally matted. Drawings, with their expanses of white space, provide a break in an otherwise heavy decorating scheme.

Drawings are sometimes supplemented by work in other media. For example, watercolors may be worked into a drawing, and you have what is described as a wash and line drawing. One marvelous German artist, named Lyonel Feininger, distinguished himself working in this style. Another German artist, Fritz Busse, worked in this style and illustrated several remarkable books on American cities, which were sold inexpensively in Boston, New York, Washington, San Francisco, and New Orleans—cities on which these art books were based. Gift shops offered framed and laminated reproductions from the books at low prices. Since drawings are usually in one color, reproductions are easy to turn out. Some are so good that even experts experience difficulty distinguishing them from originals.

Rembrandt used his various etching techniques to give the impression of light and shadow in **Faust.**

Although drawings by famous artists may command high prices, they do not often touch the prices of oils or watercolors.

Many painters in oils and other media draw preliminary sketches prior to working on their canvases or paper or etching plate or lithographic stone. These sketches are often saved and offered in galleries. These sketch-drawings are relatively low-priced and offer collectors of modest means opportunities to buy work by prominent artists.

Original Graphics

Most important of the original graphics are etchings, lithographs, silk screens and pochoir, wood cuts and wood engravings, and steel engravings. These, with the frequent exception of steel engravings, may be in limited editions or unlimited, or a combination of the two systems.

Etchings. Of all the kinds of original graphics, etchings demand of the artist the most skill, patience, and hard work.

A plate, usually zinc, is covered with a form of wax, or some similar ground, and the artist draws into it with a needle-like instrument, thus uncovering the metal underneath wherever he wants the line of the design to go. The design is bitten into the exposed lines when the plate is immersed into an acid bath. Because the artist can draw into the wax almost as readily as he can draw with a pencil, he has freedom to work without restraint. He can make wider or subtler lines, or heavy backgrounds by skillful use of his needle-like instrument.

While many etchings are of one color, with shades achieved by techniques available to the artist, multiple-color etchings are also made. This is done by etching one plate for each color and carefully controlling the overprinting of each with the aid of small marks on the plate to indicate where the plates are to be lined up in order to lay the successive colors right on the mark.

A related technique, called aquatint, permits tonal variations, and more subtle coloring and shading. This is achieved by depositing fine granules of a resinous material on the plate in such a way that the fine granules are used where finer gradations are desired; and where coarser ones are desired, the granules are altered. If the artist desires a white area, he puts an acid resistant material over these granular-grounds to prevent acid etching; this means no ink will be held on the plate in the printing operation, and the space so treated will show up white.

Several other techniques closely related to etching are used by artists. All of these techniques, including etching and aquatint, are known under the general term *intaglio.*

The one related method requiring brief mention is steel engraving, which differs by having the design cut right into the metal plate. Although some fine steel engravings have been made, they lack the delicacy and fine shading possible with some of the techniques. Before modern printing was developed, steel engravings were widely used for book and magazine illustrations. Many famous artists produced them, notably Winslow Homer as an artist-correspondent for *Harper's Magazine* during the Civil War. Plates made by artists who later became famous have been resurrected by enterprising publishers, and even some museums. These are called restrikes.

Over the years these plates undoubtedly have been worked until the handiwork of the original artist has been long removed from them. However, some interesting and sometimes inexpensive restrikes of great names like Rembrandt's, can be bought. At places like the Bibliotheque Nationale in Paris, restrikes of many famous European artists can be obtained at reasonable prices.

It's important that you remember that these are available, because there are charlatans gulling the gullible with representations that the Rembrandt etchings are original Rembrandts, made by his hand. They would then, of course, be very valuable.

One way to tell if you have an etching or related intaglio print is by feeling the slight depression where ink has been deposited. This results from the pressure of the roller into the depression where the ink was deposited. You will also notice an elevation around the edge of the print, indicating that the entire paper was forced into the plate. If you fail to spot these signs, then you may have a photo-mechanical reproduction of an etching. If the seller claims this is a real etching, walk out of the gallery or emporium and call the nearest Better Business Bureau or Consumer Protection Agency.

Lithographs. Every schoolchild knows that water and oil won't mix. That simple principle led to the development of lithography, which is now one of the most popular graphic methods.

Originally, a lithograph artist would draw his design on a special kind of stone found only in a single deposit in Bavaria; he would use a greasy crayon or an oily ink for the design. The stone would accept water where the dried oily material was absent. A wet sponge was wiped over the stone, leaving a wet surface where the stone had no greasy design. To put color into the design and transfer it to paper for the finished lithograph, an oily paint or ink was rolled over the entire stone. Since oil does not stick to a water moistened surface, only the design made of the greasy crayon picks up the ink or paint.

Once the design had been set in ink, a piece of paper was placed over the stone, and the stone and paper were run through a press, usually by hand, to impress the design on to paper and create a lithograph.

In recent years, because the Bavarian stone deposit is running out, designs have been drawn on zinc plates, and even on treated plastic.

As with etchings, lithographs can be made in multiple colors. By preparing a stone for each color and then overprinting with the aid of index marks, the impression of each color will fall just where the artist planned.

And even more than etchings, lithographs can be misrepresented. Original lithographs, as we said about all original graphics, are either made by the artist's hand, under his direction, or at least with his approval. Until the 1950s original lithographs were always made on hand-operated and hand-controlled presses.

Now, some so-called official organizations—such as graphic art associations—have started to regard machine-printed lithographs as original if the artist either draws the plates himself or sanctions the drawings and the impressions.

These machine-printed lithographs, often printed from zinc "stones" instead of real Bavarian stones, come out uniformly; they don't have the individual differences that hand-rolled lithographs show as a result of flattening of the inked-design or the pressure variation applied by the craftsman-printer.

Although they are uniform and look printed, work made by lithograph-like techniques are sometimes sold to the unsuspecting consumer for high prices.

Wary buyers should beware of a favorite ploy of art tradesmen, as distinguished from reputable dealers. They buy up art magazines reproduced in France, or catalogs for art shows produced by one or another of these mass-reproduction methods, and then cut out the pictures, frame them and sell them as unnumbered original lithographs. This is done very often by private auctioneers brought in by churches and clubs for fundraising. Low-value works by some big name artists—such as Picasso, Braque, Chagall, Rouault, Miro, Friedlander, and Steinberg, to name a few—have been sold in this manner for prices in excess of $100. The magazines from which they come, *Verve, Derriere La Miroir,* were bought for as little as $3 each per copy, and some carry as many as 10 "lithographs."

The means of identifying a lithograph is its continuous tone quality. Continuous tone indicates that the colors and shadings are registered on the paper from printing plates that deposit ink in a continuous manner, rather than in tiny dots, as is done in common offset printing used for most mass-production magazines. So, check the lithograph you are considering under a magnifying glass for dots. However, even if the print has no dots it is not necessarily a lithograph, original or otherwise. Here's a second test; rub your finger lightly over the edge and near the edge of the printed portion of the paper to see if you can feel a slight elevation of ink above the surface. A lithograph printed by a craftsman or an artist on a true lithographic press should have ink you can feel. Mass-production methods deposit ink more uniformly and leave a flatter surface. Another (fallible) indication of an original graphic is the paper it's on. Most use water-marked paper which, unfortunately, can be bought by men with fakery in their hearts as well as by honest art-printers. The "Arches" watermark (pronounced ARSH), is found on the most popular of the quality lithograph papers. The "Japon Nacre" mark shows up on finer quality work, most commonly very small editions or small hand-signed portions of larger editions.

Lithographs, and etchings as well, may have one of several kinds of pencil-markings at their lower left, below the actual picture. These are supposed to indicate the number of copies made and the number of the copy at hand. The number or fraction (10/30) means theoretically that you are holding the tenth print out of a total of 30 produced. It usually means that you have the tenth one that the artist signed and numbered.

If the fraction is in Roman numerals, such as IX/XXV, that usually means a special edition, possibly on special paper, was run off before the larger edition was made. Very often, this special run will be signed in pencil by the artist. If the artist is famous, the likelihood is that these special, hand-signed prints will be considered more valuable than those numbered later in Arabic numerals. The latter may be on some less prestigious paper, probably Arches, while those with roman numerals might be on finer paper, such as Japon Nacre.

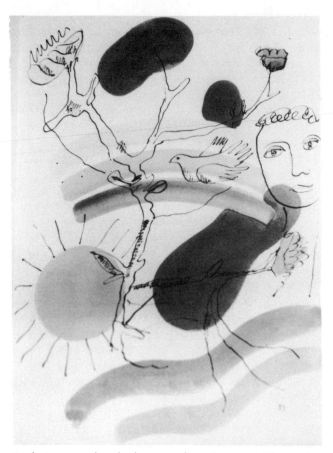

Pochoir, a stencil method, was used to color Leger's lithographs.

Fine art is often reproduced in silk screen. Here, a painting by Georges Braque (courtesy of Art for Art's Sake Gallery, N.Y.).

Moreover, sometimes prints marked with Arabic numerals will not be hand-signed in pencil by the artist, but will be signed on the stone. This means his signature will be printed as part of the lithograph itself, rather than as an autograph. Still further editions may be made without any signature at all. In addition, the artist is usually allowed to keep 10 or so copies.

The hand-signed editions, the signed-on-the-stone edition, the artist's proofs, the unsigned, and the unnumbered editions—all are virtually the same picture, except for some minor and often imperceptible change in quality as more prints are made, or if different paper is used. Japon Nacre paper, for example, is not merely a matter of prestige; it adds to the appearance of the print because of the way it takes ink and gives a subtle lustre. Arches paper also provides the look of quality, while some garden variety paper used on unnumbered editions may actually detract.

Whenever you buy a print, insist on knowing the size of the edition. If it was a signed edition, learn how many were signed, how many artists' proofs were made, and how many unsigned prints were issued. The more rare, the more valuable it is. Also remember that a good print, a really fine one in a large edition, may well be more valuable than a poor work of art in a small edition.

The safest bet is to select what pleases you. Still, even when pleased don't let a salesman overcharge you once he sees that you like the print. Let him know you know about signed editions and numbers, and so on, and he is less likely to try to inflate his prices.

A reputable gallery (always buy higher priced art from a *reputable* gallery) will be able to tell you something else about the print: does it come from a set of prints, sometimes referred to as a portfolio. Occasionally an important artist will make a set based on some theme. It may be to illustrate a famous book. Marc Chagall did a series on the Bible, published in a single edition. The themed groups are usually bought by collectors and museums, and also art galleries. The latter frequently break up the portfolios and sell individual prints, making more money that way than by selling entire portfolios. Some of the individual pictures from sets by famous artists come on the market from time to time and bring lots of money. Hand-signed prints bring even more. For example, unnumbered prints from the "Bible" that appeared in a limited-edition French art magazine, *Verve*, brought hundreds of dollars.

If you believe the print offered you comes from a portfolio, insist on seeing the *justification,* which is a description of the edition, such as the number of the different kinds of prints made, the artist, the printer, the subject, date of creation, etc. If the seller doesn't have the justification, that means he's far down on the list of those handling the print. He probably bought it from someone who in turn bought it from someone who may have broken up the portfolio. If he is a sound print dealer, he will at least have information from the justification, or know how to get it.

What about price? You don't have to pay a fortune for delightful and potentially valuable lithographs or etchings. You can buy, for $40 to $150, perfectly fine art works by artists who 10 years from now may be big names.

Silk Screen and Pochoir. A common name can be assigned these two related art forms: stencil method. The silk screen, also called a serigraph, is made from a stencil on a field of finely meshed silk. A pochoir (pronounced pushwar), produced mainly in France, is printed from a stencil made by cutting out the desired design in a thin, nonporous material, such as treated paper, metal, or plastic. Ink is rolled through openings produced in the silk of the serigraph or in the cutout portion of the pochoir stencil.

For silk screens, the process is more complicated. The meshed silk is spread tightly onto a frame. A stop-out material, called *tusche,* is painted on by the artist wherever he wants the design to be transferred to the paper. The entire screen is then covered with a material that will not allow ink to pass through the screen and onto paper.

Then the tusche is removed, with refined kerosene, leaving a clear area in the silk so ink can pass through and be transferred to the paper. Ink is applied by roller. By superimposing additional colors on the first impression, multicolor designs can be produced.

Silk screens, in the pecking order of fine art prints, are not as highly regarded as etchings or lithographs. For one thing, just about any artist can learn in a very short while how to make them. Still, many great artists have produced them, or have had their work reproduced for them by artisan serigraphers. Numerous books have been illustrated with stencil-derived prints, particularly in pochoir. Some of them have become valuable.

Wood Cuts and Wood Engravings. To understand how these prints are made, we need only to look at a rubber stamp, with its figures and words standing clearly visible above a cut-out area. This is known as relief printing. Whereas the ink for the printing of an etching settles in a depression and pressure on the paper forces it into the inked depression, in relief printing the ink remains on the elevated areas, which have the design.

To make a woodcut, the artist draws on a piece of smooth hardwood. He, or a wood carver, then cuts out everything around the area marked. This leaves the design elevated, or in relief. The artist, or a printer, then inks the high portion—the design—and applies sufficient

The Paul Honore woodcuts illustrating this edition make this a very valuable book. Books can be set up on stands on shelves for better display.

pressure on paper to pick up the ink.

Woodcuts often have the additional benefit of including some of the natural wood grain.

Some of the most beautiful and widely distributed wood cuts are sensitive versions that came from Japan many years ago. They show volcanoes, temple gardens, kimonoed ladies, and relaxing men and children. These woodcuts, as it happens, were credited with inspiring many of the famous French Impressionists.

Wood engravings use the same principle as the woodcut, but vary in two particulars: first, the design is cut into the end-block of hard wood, which is actually a cross section cut across the grain. This provides an extremely hard surface that permits making many impressions; second, the artist aims for a design in white on a black background, rather than a black design on a white background. He achieves this by reversing the area that he cuts out. For a woodcut, he cuts out what is not to appear in the design. In other words, he cuts out the background. For a wood engraving, on the other hand, he cuts out what will be the design, and the ink on the remaining elevated part of the block supplies what is a black background for the white design created on the paper by absence of ink.

Neither the woodcuts nor wood engravings are regarded as highly as lithographs or etchings, although some are widely collected and held in high esteem. Mostly, however, these are used for illustrating books Some woodcuts or wood engravings from old books have

Abstract painting sets off the design in the geometric foil wall covering (Lis King photo).

considerable value, the books themselves even more so. One book, illustrated in wood engravings by Thomas Bewick, *History of English Birds,* is of great value. Fritz Eichenberg, probably the most famous contemporary wood engraver, illustrated numerous limited edition books, which have become collectors' items, particularly those illustrating Dostoievsky and Tolstoy.

Photo-Mechanical Reproductions

Letter Press. The relief printing method, as described for woodcuts and engravings, is also used for a mass production method of printing known as *letter press.*

In many cases letter press has been replaced by offset printing (which uses photo chemical means). But the letter press, or direct printing method, is still used effectively for printing decorative art. In general, better printing can be done by offset, but if the number of prints is small it may not pay to go to the expense of offset and letter press may be used effectively for art of 2, 3 or more colors.

One of the steps in offset or letter press is the placing of a fine screen in front of the lens through which the exposure is made. The actual image that ends up on the printing plate is broken up by the screen into fine dots. These dots are there to hold the ink that is to go on the printing paper. Using screens permits various degrees of shading, and when used with color, it aids in making a full color plate with only four primary colors and black.

The finer the dot, usually, the closer is the printing to the original picture. Letter press, or relief printing, for a number of reasons, cannot use as fine a screen on its plates as does offset printing.

Offset. Offset printing is photo-mechanical lithography with an added step: placing the ink on the paper from a rubber blanket, which picks up the ink from the metal plate. The plate has been given the design in an oily paint or heavy ink, which rejects water but, even when it hardens, accepts printing ink as it's rolled on.

Because the rubber blanket gives the ink an opportunity to dry somewhat before it hits the paper, very fine screens can be used on the plate (see section on Letter Press), permitting the transfer of fine details in the art. The blanket and partial drying prevent smearing of ink on the fine screen.

Low-priced prints for framing are most often produced by offset. These are frequently reproductions of famous art works for which the demand is expected to be strong. Companies specialize in producing these under license from museums or individual collections. These prints can be bought for as little as a dollar, and as much as a hundred dollars if they are modified by hand work so that they seem to have brush strokes or other signs of an artist's work.

Companies in recent years have been taking high-quality offset prints and, with the aid of sophisticated computerized equipment, have been depositing heavy paint-like materials on them to simulate the original painting. By law these must differ dimension-wise from the original to prevent misrepresentation.

Photo-gravure. Prints made by some types of photo-gravure are more highly regarded than those by offset. Of all the mass-produced prints offered, those by a process known as *sheet-fed gravure* are the finest, all things otherwise being equal, such as the quality of the original art.

Gravure has certain features that resemble etchings; ink for the impressions is deposited in depressions. In photo-gravure the design is transferred from a negative to the photo-sensitive plate by a costly process that requires skilled craftsmen. So photo-gravure requires expensive preparatory work; hence, it is usually used for large runs that can justify the big investment in skilled labor. Also, some art book publishers use it for extra-fine art, when they resort to sheet-fed gravure. Paper for high-quality gravure is fed in single sheets on special presses.

For mass-produced magazines, such as Sunday supplements, rotary gravure presses are used. This is called rotogravure, and because the presses run so fast and ink-

Collotype reproductions in this room are so good they could be taken for originals (Lis King photo). Paisley wall paper gives elegant touch against wood moldings and fine furniture.

ing is so hard to control, quality of printing is inferior to sheet fed.

Collotype. If photo-gravure resembles etchings, collotype has much in common with lithographs, because it depends on the ability of oily materials to reject water and welcome oil. Two differences are the material used for the plate, which in this case is glass or plastic, and the method of transferring the design. In collotypes, a photomechanical method is used.

A few high-priced print publishers still use collotype, which usually commands a higher price than offset or gravure. Very often, large museums contract to have reproductions of their most important and most popular art produced by collotype. These can be distinguished by the absence of dots under a magnifying glass, which may cause them to be confused with lithographs or silk screen. Each color requires its own plate, unlike offset, which achieves some colors by combining primary colored dots. As many as 12 or 15 plates may be needed to make a fine collotype, which is one reason they are more costly than other reproductions.

Silk Screens. Under original prints, silk screens were described, along with pochoir. These versions were made by or under supervision of the originating artists. Photomechanical silk screens, or *serigraphs,* of original art are also offered.

Popular-priced silk screens are usually made in smaller editions than the foregoing photo-mechanically produced offset and gravure prints, and often they are less complicated than those made by the other methods. Photo-mechanically produced silk screens are without dots on the surface, and like collographs, may be mistaken for lithographs. Some excellent silk screens, with one screen used for each color, are offered at reasonable prices.

Many posters are produced in silk screen, as well as by offset. Smaller editions of posters, and other art, are less expensive to print by silk screen than by offset because the screens can be made more quickly and less expensively.

Popular posters, such as those announcing exhibitions by Picasso, Braque, Leger, Toulouse Lautrec, Chagall and other great names, have been produced by silk screen, as well as by other photo-mechanical processes. Originally posters of that kind were done in lithography, with the artist's supervision, when he wasn't the

35

actual printer. Original posters such as these, regardless of the method used, are growing in value.

Some excellent silk screen reproductions are to be found, as well as some poor ones. The buyer must exercise judgment in his selection, and should be on guard against buying silk screens that are offered as lithographs. Once again, reliable galleries can be depended on. Buying elsewhere is always risky.

Black and White and Color Photography. Before photography became commonplace, artists had seen its possibilities as a fine art form. Many so-called salon prints of the turn-of-the-century are now collectors items of great value.

And later in the century, successful, widely known artists—notably Man Ray and the great Steichen, whose *Family of Man* collection is a popular classic, proved conclusively that photography, with the right photographer behind the lens, is a form of fine art.

Today almost every college with a fine arts department offers courses in photographic techniques; also, every museum of art worthy of the name has its collection of fine photographic art.

Photographs come in black and white, and in color. For a number of reasons, black and white is more challenging to the photographer. The main reason is that the color photographer sees what will, to a great extent, show up in his developed picture or slide. A black and white photographer has to think in terms of film sensitivity to color—whether the reds, for instance, will turn out as black or white or some intermediate gradation between black and white. Similarly most of the other colors have to be accounted for on a scale of black and white. Each color absorbs certain components of light and bounces the remainder back to our eyes as the color we see. When this colored reflection reaches a sensitive black and white film, it is picked up in accordance with the color sensitivity of the film. Some films are blind to red, so red shows up virtually as black. If the color is light red, the film is a little less blind so the film picks up a little light, and then we have light red translated by the film into a gradation of black. The black and white photographer has to know this, and he can bring out light reds and make them even blacker by using a red filter over his camera lens. With that same red filter he can make clouds stand out very clearly; under some conditions he can make an outdoor picture's clouds seem as if they were captured at night.

With a green filter he can heighten greens, particularly if he is using a film blind to green. He can also emphasize blues and make clouds and sky stand out, but not quite as strongly as a red filter can. With yellow filters he can darken the image of yellows, greens and blues, and give a gentler emphasis to clouds.

So the photographer with black and white film can use artistry with his filters, and he can use light from the sun or from spotlights or floodlights, or available room lights to emphasize features and focus attention on centers of interest.

Color photography, with film sensitive to virtually all colors, may be less challenging to the photographer. By being at the right place at the right time with a reasonably good camera, anyone can luck a good picture—particularly with modern cameras that do all the thinking as to exposure, speed and focus; nonetheless, fine color photos can add much to a decorative arrangement, and will, no doubt, have more appeal than all but the most skillfully produced black and white.

Some of these works are distinguished by their subject matter and the skill with which they were shot and then processed in the laboratory. Many of these are realistic, or representational photography. Other photographic prints are partly representational and partly abstract, and still others are surreal. Some photos are totally divorced from reality. Still others are pictures of actual scenes or objects but have been given a gently softened effect by use of a diffusing lens in addition to the regular lens. Sometimes a slightly blurred effect is achieved by having the lens slightly out of focus. The blurred and softened pictures often closely resemble painted art, particularly if the prints are matted and framed.

Recognizing Desirable Art

Personal Reaction. Whoever buys art has a right to select what pleases him. If you have seen lots of good art and have had an opportunity to cultivate taste for works that also attract other persons with broad experience, your choices may have dollar value as well as personal value.

So what do you do when you haven't seen enough art to know if there's inspiration or skill? And what do you do if you haven't developed a taste beyond calendar art? Or suppose you honestly like pretty nudes, and contented cows grazing by tree-draped lazy-flowing rivers at sunset?

You can do several things, some better than others, but better than settling for schlock art.

First, you can enlist the aid of a decorator. If he or she is certified, he will either be informed about kinds of art and have a fair decorative sense, or be starving at his trade.

On the other hand, many if not most decorators are primarily interested in harmonizing color schemes and balancing parts of a room. This is also highly valuable.

Even better are the services of a dependable gallery owner recommended by a friend who has had good results, or by a museum curator.

Flat, angular, carved, scratched, plain, stained, and painted— molding frames come in many forms (Glenn photo).

PICTURE FRAMES

A frame should be selected considering both the picture it will be used on and the wall behind the picture.

Here are some of the reasons we use frames:

1. To direct the eye to the picture itself and help hold it there.
2. To help strengthen underlying values in the picture and its sometimes elusive color elements.
3. To give more dimension to the picture.
4. To provide a transition from the picture to the wall behind it.

Make certain that the design and colors of the picture harmonize with your wall covering; no frame can overcome such a conflict. If you have a gay floral design on the wall, you must carefully select a frame that will prevent the wallpaper from stealing attention from the art. With a flowery wall covering, your painting will fail to get attention unless it has strong, attention-getting colors in it. Your frame should be selected to serve in isolating the picture from the background.

Selecting a frame more often than not is left up to the frame dealer. You may leave it entirely up to him; just give him the facts about your room, your wall, and the other elements of your decor—furniture, piano, rug, etc. Or you can come to your frame-maker informed by the basics outlined here, and you can make certain that the artisan really knows his business, and that your tastes are the deciding factor.

The frames you buy can contribute much to the decoration of your room. An unfortunate selection can destroy the color and pictorial value of your work of art, and cancel out your decorative intentions, which were to enhance the wall or walls where the picture is to hang.

Frames for valuable pictures should usually be bought at shops capable of doing justice to them. For inexpensive reproductions or glass-fronted watercolors, pastels, or prints, ready-made frames are often suitable. These are turned out by mass production methods, with electric choppers slicing lengths of molding into suitably sized pieces already angled at the ends and ready for joining. Workmen put the corners into special holders and giant staple guns secure them. A good man can turn out a frame in two minutes or less.

Staple holes are then covered with caulk, and the frames are sprayed, dried, and packed.

Molding Types

Just as we said that art should be bought from highly recommended, established dealers, frames for the picture of your choice should be bought from an established shop.

Selecting a frame for a picture is sometimes an art in itself, although basic guidelines are available so you will have, at least, something to help you get started.

Against an attention-getting background of flowers and fabric nosegays, the mantel needs a strong picture and frame to help direct the eye to it (wall covering by W.H.S. Lloyd, Inc.; window-shades by Joanna Western Mills; Hilda Sachs photo).

Two different moldings are used here, taking care that the pictures harmonize with the foil background, the fireplace, and the potentially overwhelming clock.

Many considerations enter into frame selection. Is it for a romantic picture? Does the picture have motion, either of objects or animated beings, or possibly "motion" of lines, such as diagonals crisscrossing or moving? Is it a structure? Large, or small, far from the foreground or near? Is it of a small child, or a rugged man, or of some person of intermediate pictorial weight? These are some of the questions one should ask in deciding on the width and heft of the molding.

The questions cited above have to do with pictorial "weight" and its relation to the molding. Romantic pictures and those of children are termed "light"; pictures of rugged men and architectures are described as "heavy." Intermediate weight would be represented by larger children and ornately dressed men and women.

The reasons for varying heft of moldings are obvious. A romantic scene of two lovers on a piano bench might look lost in a wide, ornate frame. Conversely, wouldn't a picture of a rugged fisherman tugging at his nets look unfinished with a thin molding around it?

The picture frame is like a window, through which we see a picture, just as a window frames the landscape.

In fact, frames and pictures, until the Renaissance of the 1400s in Italy, were regarded as windows onto a scene, and as part of a room's architecture. Originally, most of them were three-sided, like the molding around a door.

A rebellion against that sort of demeaning attitude toward pictures was staged by artists of the period. They demanded that paintings be given separate status. They began making their own frames and insisted that both their creations be kept together.

Over the years a few molding styles, with many variations, have evolved. They are as follows:

1. Flat (or angular);
2. Mono-curved (one curve);
3. Multi-curved;
4. Combination (curves and angles).

These descriptions, of course, refer to the width of the molding. In addition to these basic edge-to-edge shapes, moldings are decorated with carvings, or scratchings, or may have metallic or stone ornaments affixed to them. Lower-priced moldings have mock-carvings produced by shaping plastic or gesso materials.

Finally, moldings have a finish of some kind, either visible or invisible. The visible finishes are paint, stain, gold or silver metallic leaf, and bronze powder coatings that are used to simulate gold leaf. These visible finishes can also be combined with paint on one part of the surface; for example, paint with gold leaf as a highlight. Some moldings are multi-colored.

Invisible finishes are there for protection. They preserve the natural surface of the molding, when that is

Watercolors, pastels and most prints and reproductions are set off by a pressed-paper mat. Used with wall covering, mats strengthen the separation of picture and background (wall covering by Columbus Coated Fabrics).

Colored mats intensify picture colors. The calm, uncluttered art work both complements and contrasts with the dramatic and foil wall covering by Columbus Coated Fabric (Lis King photo).

Two Types of Thin Brick Finishes suitable for interior accent: at left, individual "Hearth Brick" wall covering units applied with adhesive are 3/16-inch thick, of mineral composition and have the texture and fire-resistance of real bricks. These thin units are made

by the GAF Corp. and are applied without mortar fill for the joints. At right, fiberglass-reinforced molded bricks in panel form made by Masonite's Roxite division. The panels have invisible seams, are available in choice of colors and may be used inside or out.

attractive. Oak, for example, is often covered with a preserving finish, such as varnish, shellac, or wax.

As part of certain types of frames—mainly those used for water colors, pastels, and prints—mats are used. These are usually made of pressed paper. Their outer dimensions allow them to fit in a frame. Their inner dimensions permit a slight overlap of the picture. Mats may be white or colored, or may be covered with cloth or textured material.

Assembling Your Own

Some firms and other framing specialists offer prints ready for your wall. Many of these framed prints are priced entirely out of line with the value of the frames. Unframed prints, or prints with mats already affixed, can be bought more advantageously if unpainted frames are bought at art or paint stores and assembled at home.

The mass-produced chopped moldings can be bought unassembled. You join them yourself, paint them, and save considerable money. For this you will need a vise, or some device for holding the corners prior to nailing them.

In addition, aluminum unassembled frames, with simulated silver or gold finish (usually by anodizing) are also offered at art stores and many paint stores. These are

satisfactory for many matted pictures able to take a narrow molding. They are easier to assemble than chopped wood molding, since they are joined by screws placed in previously cut holes. No vise is needed.

The buyer thus has a choice in buying or assembling his own frames. The kind of picture involved will influence the kind of frame selected, whether or not you wish to assemble a frame, buy a ready-made frame, or order a custom frame.

STONE, BRICK, AND MIRROR VENEERS

Real ceramic brick and stone, in thinner-than-usual units, and real mirrors in square and rectangular units, are easy to apply. They broaden the decorating choices open to the do-it-yourselfer.

Brick and Stone

Standard rectangular brick units as well as antiqued and irregular rustic styles are furnished in 5/16" thickness to facilitate application. Random-size fieldstone of the same thickness in white, brown, and granite gray is also offered.

These are not simulated but are made of the actual

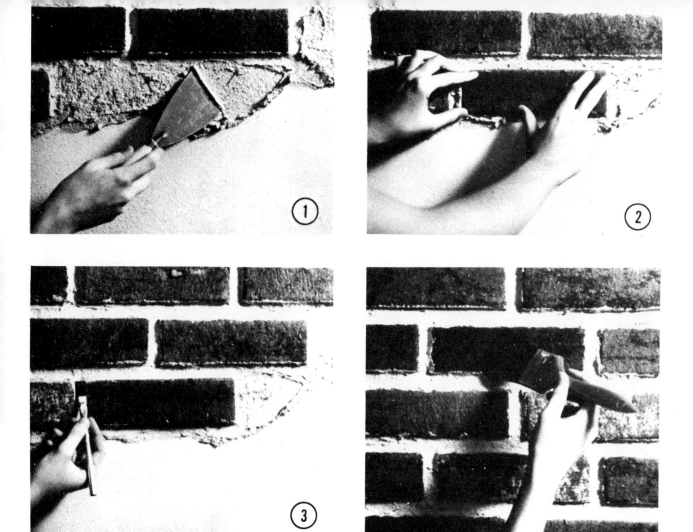

Thin Brick Installation using bricks, adhesive and sealer made by the Z-Brick Company. Steps are: (1) spread ⅙ inch coat of mortarlike adhesive; (2) press brick into place wiggling, slightly to seat; (3) smooth adhesive between bricks with narrow brush; (4) apply one or two coats of sealer to make surface washable.

material, so that when you decorate with them you end up with a realistic effect. Although not as thick as conventional material, the products are made the same way.

Home centers and decorative merchandising stores where these Z-Bricks and other brands are sold also stock a mortar-like adhesive that you simply trowel on. To cut the brick or stone, simply score it and snap it as you would a vinyl tile.

Mirror Tiles

Mirror tiles, either plain, bronzed, etched, swirled, or overprinted, have been added in recent years to help the decorator, professional, or do-it-yourselfer.

Fortunately, these versatile decorating products are easily applied. At least one version of a mirror tile can be bent for use with curved forms. Cutting to work around objects on the wall or windows is easy; simply use an inexpensive glass cutter.

The oldest form of mirror tile is a clear mirror one foot square. This has now been supplemented with a line of smoked, veined and antique mirrors, as well as wood-grained mirrors. Also, clear mirrors have been decorated with Mediterranean grilles and Florentine overprints. The square mirror tiles can also be obtained with solid red, blue, orange, yellow, lime or black corners surrounding a clear circle.

Antique effects have been imparted to mirrors via a patented foil treatment, and this effect is heightened by creating swirls. Such mirrors are offered in chrome, gold, blue, red, green, and yellow.

The effect of a mirror-backed wall covering can be achieved with new mirror tiles offering prints of daisies in several sizes, or ferns, moonflowers, trellises, a kaleidoscope, etc. The color schemes are earth tones, primary colors, and a combination described as lite-bright. Like the clear mirror-tiles, printed tiles are 12″ x 12″.

A decorative wallhanging and a mirror hold their own and break up this strong, warm Birge wall covering. They play an important role in setting off the period table, and creating an atmosphere.

Art and a print (on the right) are sealed to a flat board and laminated to a clear vinyl protective facing. Note that the lighting fixture coordinates with the Sanitas/Formica wall covering (New Gramercy Park photo).

The bendable tiles now offered in 12″ x 12″ sheets are really tiny mirrors separated by crisscrossing lines that provide flexibility and make them easy to cut or to conform to curves or irregular surfaces.

Clear mirror tiles and most of the decorated tiles are also available in 2″ x 6″ tiles.

OF SCONCES, EAGLES, PLAQUES, AND THREE-DIMENSIONAL DOODADS

Variety shops and elegant decorator shops carry numerous supplementary decorating materials for wall treatments. They range from odd-ball pieces to many of considerable dignity. Intelligently used they can break a somewhat flat sequence of pictures by providing a third-dimension. They can also be used for wall groupings.

Items include low-relief sculptures, candle-simulating sconces, American eagles, and everything between. These, like pictures, should be put up only after considering their effect on the rest of the room. Their colors should not fight with the wall, particularly if a bright, lively wall covering is used, and they should not be so close to a framed picture that the picture loses its power.

Wall plaques with mottos or designs can be made quite easily from magazine cutouts or from travel material picked up on trips or from travel agencies. They can be pasted to plywood paneling or to flat or rough wood, smoothed at the place reserved for the cutout. For protection and to make them sparkle, a clear varnish can be brushed, rolled, or sprayed on.

Sconces, eagles, plaques, and other miscellaneous doodads should be used sparingly. Plaques probably lend themselves to more general use than the others because they are two-dimensional and fit right in with framed pictures. In fact, pictures can be placed on plaques instead of in frames, but this should only be done on a limited scale, unless economy demands it.

Chagall's famous Jerusalem Windows have been reproduced in offset and are laminated to vinyl and plywood.

Paneling and Rigid Wall Coverings

WOOD-FACED SURFACES

Until about 35 years ago, special carpentry skills were needed when installing wood-faced materials. And until that time, the only wood facings available were various kinds of lumber, usually in planks or boards.

With the coming of wood in plies—slices of wood laid one atop another and cemented—facings of beautiful, exotic woods that previously could have been bought by few families, were brought within reach of just about everyone. Most homes, previously limited to commonplace inexpensive woods such as pines of various kinds, can now afford thin slices of cherry, mahogany, beech, walnut, or chestnut to serve as facings. Lesser varieties provide bulk and solidity behind the plywood coverings.

Plywood is offered in thicknesses ranging from ⅛ inch to about ¾ inch. If you are planning to decorate an existing wall with plywood, then a ⅛ inch material will be suitable; if you are putting the wood directly over studs, so that plywood will become the wall, then you should have at least ¼ inch, preferably ½ inch. For fire safety, you should back up thin plywood paneling with ½ inch of gypsum board. This helps prevent flash fires.

In addition to plywood, you can also use particleboard with either printed or laminated facings. This utilizes waste-wood, which is pulverized and mixed with liquid plastic to be formed into board under pressure, creating a strong, durable product.

Since plywood and particleboard, in addition to their decorative roles, also provide heat and sound insulation, it follows that the thicker the panel you select, the more effective will be its insulative value.

These materials are bought in panels, usually 4 feet x 8 feet. They are cut with a saw and may be nailed or stapled. For those who prefer to work with adhesive, they may be placed on the wall with adhesive and a minimum amount of nailing.

Application

When applying plywood, it is advisable to have a hammer, a hand or electric saw, a steel square, a rule, a level and a plumb line.

Measure your rooms, as you would for flexible wall covering, and allow another 5 to 10 percent for damaged areas or bad matching. Excess can be used for trimming cabinets or making boxes.

Let your panels sit a few days so they can do whatever shrinking they're liable to do. Pile them face to face and back to back, with a 2 x 4 separating every eight panels so they won't curl.

Before starting to apply them, buy finish nails. These can be set in and then finished off with the aid of a countersink so the board won't be marred. You may also be able to buy colored nails; otherwise, putty colored the same as the facing can be used to cover the countersink nail holes.

If you're going directly to the studs, use 1-inch nails. If you're going over furring or backerboard, use 1⅝ inch.

Instead of using conventional nails, an easier way is to buy a nail gun, which operates like a stapling device.

No matter which method you use for fastening, be certain you have a level surface. If the wall is not level, furring strips should be added to the depressed areas so that your facings will be level when you apply them.

Remove all moldings and baseboard from finished walls you are re-covering; use this trim again, if you wish. Locate the studs with a magnetic stud finder so that your nails will be on the supporting members. Or drill holes until experiencing resistance indicating presence of the stud. Mark the floor beneath each stud with tape so you will know where to drive your nails.

Before installing panels, place them around the room so you are certain they match properly. If using simulated wood grain, this will not be necessary.

Nails should be placed eight to nine inches apart

---

*apply furring horizontally around the room, adding vertical members every 16 inches, or where the panel joints occur. Horizontal spacing is usually every 2 feet.

Apply panels with care for details and caution to avoid damaging the panel prefinish. This plywood paneling installation uses Georgia Pacific panels: (1) circular electric saw for cutting but note that the panel is face down on the saw horses because the blade tips cut upwards; (2) a compass is used to trace the irregularities of adjacent brickwork thereby scribing an irregular mark on the panel which, when cut, will allow the panel to follow the contours of the bricks; (3) ⅝ or ¾ inch drill corners of a small cutout area to start, followed by a keyhole saw (4) or power jig saw to cut to the exact lines of the cutout.

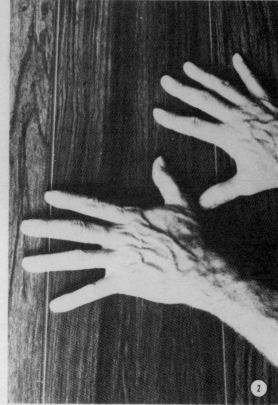

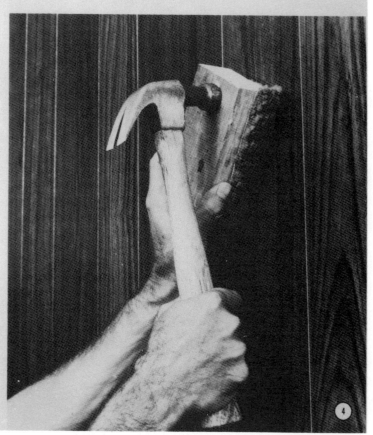

Tips for glue-up application of hardboard panelings: (1) studs or furring strips (in basement application) are first given bead of adhesive and panel is pressed into position carefully so a minimum of shifting is needed after glue contact; (2) apply uniform steady hand pressure to seat in the adhesive; (3) tack-nail with finishing nails at top of sheet leaving heads exposed for later easy removal; (4) use a padded block following a 15-to-20 minute interval to reapply pressure in a final adhesive-setting procedure. Paneling shown is the Masonite Corporation.

46

Wainscot paneling, another way of finishing walls in bathrooms and kitchen dining areas. Smoothly finished hardboard panels in wainscot size have now been packaged by Masonite's Marlite division in kit form for easier installation. The main steps are: (1) getting off to a vertical start through the use of a plumb reference line; (2) the Marlite panels are placed and held in position on the wall by the use of special edge clips; (3) a cap-mold follows panel placement to provide trim along the top edge; and (4) the completed installation gives a highly attractive yet easy-clean appearance. Applicable in dens, dining, and other rooms as well as the kitchen and bath.

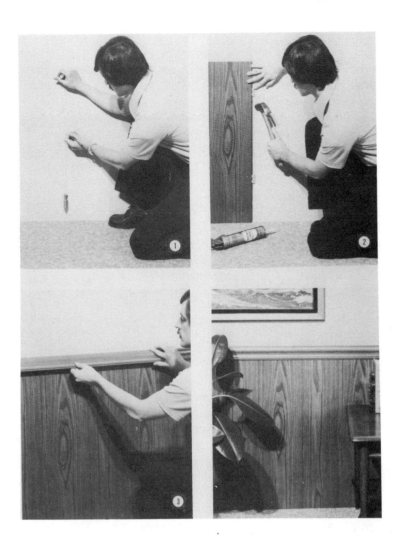

around all edges of each panel, and 12 inches apart on intermediate studs or blocks. Start the nailing either from the center and work toward the edges, or from one edge and work across to the other edge.

Do not nail both edges first, and then go to the center, because panels may buckle.

To cut out panels to fit over doors and windows, and to permit insertion of electric fixtures, use care in marking the positions where the cut is to be made. If doing all power cutting, put the face of the wood down on a smooth surface to avoid marring. The face side should be up when using a hand saw.

When preparing panels for cutouts around electric outlets, experts use a sheet of carbon paper, which is taped over the outlet. Place the panel over the area where it is to go. Tap it several times over the carbon paper, whose carbon side, of course, should be facing outward. This will result in an impression on the panel, showing where the cutout is to be made.

When putting up the first panel, use a chalk line to locate the leading edge of the panel so that it will be straight and provide a guide for succeeding panels. If the

starting corner is out of line, use a strip of masking tape near the edge of the panel to indicate the irregularity. Then take a compass and mark a line to show the section of the edge to be removed.

Flexi-Wood

In addition to plywood and particleboard, which are quite stiff, you can buy a flexible wood facing. This material, known as Flex-Wood, consists of thin plies of fine wood. So flexible is the product that it can be applied to curving surfaces. A large selection of beautifully grained woods is available. This material, however, is difficult to put up. Very few professionals can apply them, and do-it-yourselfers should stay clear of them. Only authorized Flex-Wood dealers should be trusted for application.

You can also find conventional paper, foil, or vinyl wall coverings with prints simulating various woods. These are applied like any other wall covering.

Flexible Cedar Strips

Another flexible material, one that can be applied by homeowners, is a cedar strip that is easily cut to shape and then applied to dry surfaces with any good paneling adhesive.

These cedar strips are thin enough to cut with a linoleum cutter, sharp knife, or scissors. They are flexible enough to bend around corners or curves.

The strips come in one, two, three, or four foot lengths by 3⁷/₁₆ inch wide and ¹/₉ inch thick. They are packaged in a seven lb. bundle which covers 33½ square feet, or roughly the same area covered by a 4 foot x 4 foot plywood panel.

Bundles contain light and dark strips, which means you can arrange them for a natural, warm look. You can also arrange the strips in herring-bone groupings or can use your own ingenuity to put them in artistic designs.

MOLDINGS

Moldings are, or were until recently, wood strips crafted into intricate shapes, an art introduced to the United States during the 17th century. Moldings were used to convert plain wall surfaces into paneled rooms. Before labor and material costs became so high, moldings served to conceal cracks, to protect against wall damage, and to decorate.

Moldings still offer these advantages, but higher costs have diminished their purely decorative use. Also, the wall materials used today are usually more durable than in earlier days, which reduces need for moldings even further. Moldings have come back recently in prefinished, mass-production form for more extensive, less expensive application. Metal and plastic moldings supplement unfinished wood moldings, and in some cases replace them.

Forms and Types

There are many sizes and shapes of unfinished and prefinished moldings. The two major categories are: functional and decorative. A functional molding covers and trims what would otherwise be an unsightly crack. A decorative molding is applied for its visual appeal.

There should be a relationship between the moldings selected and the places where you will use them. The molding shape names indicate, to some extent, their purposes and locations. The style of molding and the style of the home must harmonize. You should not, for example, put ornate molding in a contemporary, modernistic home; you would, on the other hand, choose traditional moldings for trimming openings of paneled doors. If your home has flush doors, use the smooth-surface or ranch-type moldings for window casings and baseboards. Try not to mix extreme molding shapes.

You will use molding trim primarily where cracks in the room need to be hidden, or to highlight particular features of a room. The areas and situations of primary use will be: paneling and tile—cap, edge, and corner trim; fireplace—wall and mantel trim.

Selection

The following moldings are generally available through lumber-supply retail outlets, and are commonly used for wall treatments.

Crown and Bed Moldings. Generally these have a curved face and edges, machined to about 60/120 degree angles. With the increasing use of gypsum wallboard and taped-cement wall-ceiling corners, their use has fallen off.

Chair Rails. Still very popular in certain areas of the home, such as dining rooms, dens, libraries, and family rooms.

Picture Moldings. Like crown-bed moldings, these go back to the days when hanging a picture meant cracking a plaster wall. The solution: a picture molding nailed through the plaster into studs near the ceiling; small copper or brass hooks were used over the moldings to hang the pictures.

Cap Molds. A relatively recent product, designed for plywood or hardboard edges. Nailed and/or glued, they give a smooth finished look.

Shelf Molding. A special wood molding with a rabbet cut in one face. The shelf board rests in this.

A wide variety of carved wood moldings for purely decorative purposes are also available.

Staining

Wood trim will take natural wood finishes. In many cases such finishing is unnecessary, since today's construction usually uses prefinished trim, and other moldings and trim sometimes have subdued grain patterns that do not lend themselves to natural finishes. However, when such finishes are needed, a wide selection is available. The old stain-plus-varnish method has in many cases given way to more specialized products. Color tints provide a considerably broader selection of wood tones than used to be the case when stains were simply based on species of wood. In addition to pigmented stain finishes, a variety of antiquing stains simulate old finishes.

OTHER WALLBOARDS

Cork

Cork is seeing more use as a wall-surfacing material as new styles, colors, and textures become available.

Useful for particular wall applications—study rooms, children's rooms, dens—it has been popular because of its ability to take thumb tacks. Two other attractive features now being recognized are its sound-deadening abilities and warm, strong appearance. Cork panels can come mounted on a backing, or can be applied with adhesive to a plywood, gypsumboard, or fiberboard backing.

Wallboards

One product increasingly more popular is a wood-fiber board with a lightly textured linen finish. It receives paint or wallpaper easily, is available in 8-foot widths and various lengths, and can be used for full wall-length installation without joints. Other fiberboard materials, some with prefinishes, are available.

Another wall product still new in its distribution is "tackboard." It was originally a commercial product sold to schools along with chalkboard, and used to tack up samples of student work. Vinyl- and burlap-covered tackboard sheets are ideal for children's rooms. Be sure to ask the manufacturer for installation instructions; they vary according to specific materials and producers.

One final type of finish should be briefly mentioned here: veneer plaster. This is a thin cement plaster coating applied over a special type of gypsumboard called "veneer base." The curing time involved in conventional plaster is eliminated, but the same sort of dense, durable, resistant surface results. And veneer plaster can be finished mirror smooth, or swirled, roughed, or otherwise textured. The application of gypsum veneer base sheets resembles that of drywall gypsumboard. The veneer plaster comes in one- and two-component systems, and is troweled on or machine-applied. The final thickness is about $1/8$ to $3/32$ inch thick. The veneer system appears to offer a reasonable cost alternative to plastering, but because considerable skills are involved it would be wise to consult and subcontract a plasterer.

BOOK SHELVES

Book shelves can be both decorative and functional, whether they are floor-to-ceiling, corner, or centered on the wall. Fine furniture stores are one source, lumber yards are another. At the latter you can purchase materials for traditional shelves, or for bricks-and-board shelves, which sit on the floor against a wall.

Items most often stored on shelves are books, phonograph records, and knick knacks. Weight on a shelf can range from only a few pounds to 50 pounds. A white pine board one inch thick will carry any such load without buckling, as long as it is supported every three feet. A 1¼ inch board would need support at five-foot intervals.

Solid-Lumber paneling is an alternative to sheet materials that is not as widely used as it once was. Shown here are narrow tongue-and-groove panels by Simpson (above) and wide rough-sawn boards known in some areas as barn boards (below).

Book Shelf Location and Design

Keep in mind when locating book shelves that they are for use as well as for show. Be certain people can get to them easily. And the light on the wall should allow easy reading of titles.

If you have a great many books, you might consider floor-to-ceiling book shelves. The bottom of the shelf begins just above the baseboards; the top shelf should be no more than six and a half feet high—any higher and no one will be able to get the books down. Floor-to-ceiling shelves have the design advantage of creating a center of interest for the room, or of framing other features in the room.

If you wish to emphasize a certain dimension of the room, such as unusual length, then long, low shelves might be just what you need. Book shelves and fireplaces make particularly attractive combinations.

Supports

The simplest shelf supports are wood cleats. They can be cut from any small board, but a one-inch width is best. Or you can use shelf molding, discussed earlier in this chapter. L-shaped shelf hangers are metal. They plug into holes drilled in the sides of book cases. The holes, in vertical rows, are spaced about two inches apart so that the shelves can be raised up or down. Shelf-support strips can be substituted for the L-shaped hangers. These narrow metal strips have horizontal slots from top to bottom. Strips are screwed to the sides of a bookcase or cabinet, and V-shaped clips are inserted into the slots for support. Shelves can be moved up and down by small degrees.

Also available are slotted metal standards for cantilevered shelves. They are, usually, long strips of metal with vertical slots from top to bottom. Metal brackets fit into the slots. They can support shelves about four to twenty inches deep, depending on the size of the brackets. Slotted standards normally screw to the wall, but there are special standards that wedge between the floor and ceiling. These enable free-standing shelves anywhere.

Shelf hardware using slotted metal channels for wall-mounting and slot-fitting metal support brackets has become quite popular for home use. Shown here, an improved shelf line by Stanley Hardware, unusual in that it can be used for double-sided application on a room divider as well as for the normal single-wall application. In lower right a close-up sketch of mounting details.

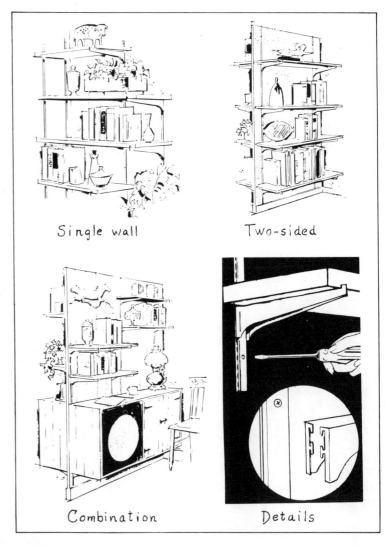

Single wall

Two-sided

Combination

Details

Light as a Decorative Component

All of what we call clear (or white) light, including the powerful rays of the sun, is actually a mixture of colored light. We see this clearly every time we look at a rainbow, or at light coming through a prism. Clear light, in these instances, has gone through a "splitter" which separates the color components that make up what we call clear light. The colors are split off into bands. The colors of our walls, or our drapes or our upholstery, are really what those objects bounce back to us from the light that falls on them.

It works this way: walls, drapes, and upholstery are colored by pigments dispersed in inks, dyes, or paint. When light falls on these pigments they absorb parts of the light; they reject the rest. What you see are the rejects —the parts of the light that objects don't absorb—all combined into what we call a color (when everything is absorbed, we have black; when everything is bounced back we have white). For example, if the rejected parts add up to what we call BLUE, we see a blue object.

The difference between the object and a rainbow or prism is the way in which they divide light. The rainbow or prism splits light into all its parts—red, yellow, blue, and green—but the object splits it into two parts. It holds on to one part, which you don't see, and it bounces back the other part and you do see it. When you see the surface of a juicy apple, for instance, it appears RED because the natural pigments in the apple absorb the blue, green, and yellow portions of the clear light falling on it and then the pigments bounce back the red portion.

What happens if the light falling on the apple has had its red component removed by a light filter? Then it can't look red because the red portion isn't there anymore; the apple will be somewhat brownish-gray. The light is now deficient in comparison to clear light.

The same sort of thing happens when light sources such as regular incandescent light bulbs or fluorescent lamps are deficient in one or more of the color compo-nents that make up clear light. And that's what this section is all about: to explain how and why you can improve your wall treatments by linking them up with the kind of lighting you have in the rooms you are decorating, or by improving your available light.

Let's start out by saying that a certain fluorescent light, known as DELUXE COOL WHITE and made by all manufacturers, comes closest in color values, among the usual sources, to natural daylight, which is the charac-teristic light at noon. Incandescent light bulbs are not quite as close. Deluxe cool whites emphasize all colors about equally. Incandescent lamps only emphasize red, orange, and yellow and make blues more blue-gray than they would be in daylight, because the amount of blue in light from an incandescent bulb is less than in Deluxe Whites. So there's less there to be radiated.

So wouldn't you think we would all want to have De-luxe Cool Whites all over the house, since they come closest to natural light? Not so. Having a fluorescent light fixture in a living, dining or bedroom is not to most people's taste. So we have mostly incandescents in our important rooms, and often find fluorescents, but not usually the Deluxe Cool Whites, in kitchens, bathrooms, laundry and workrooms.

Then, wouldn't you suppose we would avoid putting blue objects—drapes, wall covering, upholstery—under incandescents in our living, dining and bedrooms? Not at all. Blue is quite popular in these rooms.

The explanation is that widespread use of incandes-cents throughout the years has accustomed us to blues as blue-gray, and we regard the latter as natural, just as most of us like purple grape juice, which is a long way from straw-colored natural juice. If Deluxe Cool White fluor-escents had come along first, then blue-blues would have been the norm.

Now we hardly ever find Deluxe Cool Whites for sale in retail stores. The fluorescent lamps we are offered that come closest to incandescents are known as WARM WHITE. Sometimes we're only offered COOL WHITE. Warm White tends to make green and red, as well as blue, look grayish. Cool white only adds a grayish cast to red. If your fluorescent is to be blended with natural daylight, cool white is preferable. Warm white's deficiencies are partly overcome by blending with incandescent lights.

What we can learn from this is that rooms with fluorescent lamps in all probability should not had the same color scheme as rooms with incandescents, unless color differences happen not to cause one room or the other to suffer.

The other lesson is that we should select patterns in a wall-covering showroom using the same kind of light as that in the room in which the material is to go. To do otherwise means that you will not have the same effect on your wall that you have in the store.

If the lighting source is different from yours, insist on being allowed to take home a sample to check under the lighting conditions in your room. Don't be satisfied with checking the sample under the store's "Daylight Lamp," because that's not likely to be like your light, and don't take it into the daylight for the same reason.

COOL LIGHT vs. WARM LIGHT

We are all most familiar with daylight and incandescents. Daylight, for complicated reasons, emphasizes colors known as COOL COLORS. These are greens and blues, including purple-blue.

Incandescent lamps emphasize the colors known as WARM COLORS. These are yellows and reds, including red-purple. The NEUTRAL COLORS are purple, gray, and green-yellow.

Experts in color and light have found that people generally feel that strong warm colors appear to be advancing, but cool strong colors draw away or recede and help make a room seem more spacious.

Warm colors—red, orange (which is orange-red),

LAMPS AND THEIR EFFECTS ON COLOR

Lamp Names	Fluorescent Lamps						Incandescent Lamps
	Cool White	Deluxe Cool White	Warm White	Deluxe Warm White	White	Natural	Filament
Efficacy (lumens/watt)	High	Medium	High	Medium	High	Medium	Low
Lamp appearance effect on neutral surfaces	White	White	Yellowish White	Yellowish White	Pale Yellowish White	Purplish White	Yellowish White
Effect on "atmosphere"	Neutral to Moderately Cool	Neutral to Moderately Cool	Warm	Warm	Moderately Warm	Warm Pinkish	Warm
Colors Strengthened	Orange, Yellow Blue	All nearly Equal	Orange, Yellow	Red, Orange, Green, Yellow	Orange, Yellow	Red, Orange	Red Yellow, Orange
Colors Grayed	Red	None Appreciably	Blue, Green, Red	Blue	Red, Blue, Green	Green, Blue	Blue
Effects on Complexion	Pale Pink	Most Natural	Sallow	Ruddy	Pale	Ruddy Pink-Flattering	Ruddiest
Remarks	Blends with natural daylight- good color acceptance	Excellent overall color rendition	Blends with incandescent light color rendition mode	Good color rendition; simulates incandescent light	Usually replaceable with CW or WW	Tinted source usually replaceable with CWX or WWX	Good color rendering

and yellow are generally regarded as stimulating, while the cool colors—blue, blue-green, green and purple—are unexciting; green is even considered calming and quieting. If we plan our decor to achieve one or the other of these effects—stimulating or calming—and we have the wrong light source, we may defeat our purpose.

On the other hand, if we know what color we want to emphasize, we may even be able to "paint" with light to some extent.

A look at the accompanying Light and Color Harmony Chart will show that if we want to strengthen red, orange or yellow, warm colors, we should use one of the Warm White fluorescents or an incandescent bulb fixture. If we want to strengthen a cool blue or green, we should consider one of the Cool Whites. The warm lights, in other words, will flatter the warm colors, and the cool lights the cool colors.

Color experts usually recommend the warm whites and incandescents where illumination will be fairly low and where social intimacy is expected (such as dining areas or conversation circles).

Where illumination is high, and the atmosphere is crisper and more businesslike, then one of the Cool White fluorescents is preferable. (Purposely omitted are mercury vapor lamps, which are suitable for many business and industrial applications, but whose brief start-up periods make them unsuitable for homes. Also omitted here are two relatively new fluorescents, Chroma 50 and Chroma 75. The former is virtually identical to typical noon daylight, and the latter is ideal for artists' studios because it simulates the famous north light that artists seek.)

So, when arranging room decor, remember to choose colors and select lights with care, so that warm colors or cool colors will be brought out most effectively.

Using Your Photographic Exposure Meter to Determine if You Have Enough Light

Even if you have the right kind of light on your subject—incandescent, or one of the warm or cool fluorescents—how do you find out if you have sufficient light?

That's been a puzzle to a lot of people for a long time.

To answer this question I enlisted the aid of Ms. Bonnie K. Swenholt of the Photographic Technology Division, Eastman Kodak Co., Rochester, N.Y., and Mr. Howard Haynes, illumination scientist with the Illumination Engineering Society of New York City, to devise a method for using an ordinary, but reasonably accurate, photographic exposure meter to measure the illumination levels recommended by IES for various rooms and activities. These residential recommendations have in the past been set mainly for lighting engineers and are

given in foot candles, measured with costly devices not available to most people.

Although consumers do not have such instruments, they usually do have, or can borrow, ordinary photographic light meters. So we will here translate foot candles into readings on your exposure meter, as expressed in F stops, or lens openings.

The light meter in this method should be set for a film speed reading of ASA 200, with your shutter speed at $1/50$ second.

If you want a simple method, use a square of gray cardboard, or preferably a "reflecting gray card" used by professional photographers, for maximum accuracy in gauging reflected light with a meter. Place the card on the surface to be checked and hold your meter as you would to determine the light reading for taking a picture. This measures reflected light.

You can do a more accurate job if your meter measures incident light. If it does, then place the meter at the surface to be checked so you can measure the light actually reaching it, which is really what you want to find out.

If you're measuring light levels in a room as a whole, place the meter 30 inches above the floor, with the sensitive face away from the floor, and average your readings at several points.

Remember that the recommended light levels are not rigid, nor are they derived from heaven. If your reading is a little above or below the recommendation, don't be concerned. If you can't use the incident-light method and must measure reflected light, the difference is not great enough to nullify the effort.

The following chart gives lighting recommendations based on guidelines established by the Illumination Engineering Society.

ILLUMINATION LEVELS OF LIGHT

Decorated Areas	Foot Candles	Light Meter Set For 200 ASA Film Speed, at $^1/_{50}$ sec.
Living room, dining room, bedroom, family room, sun room, library	10	F1.4
Paintings and 2-dimensional art (light required)	50	F2.8
Dark paintings with fine detail	80	Midpoint F2.8-F4
Sculpture	100	F4
Entrances, hallways, stair landings	10	F1.4
Bathroom	30	F2
Shaving, makeup (on face, near mirror)	50	F2.8
Activity areas		
Kitchen, general	30	F2
Sink	70	Midpoint F2.8-F4
Range & work surfaces	50	F2.8
Laundry, general	30	F2
Ironing board	50	F2.8
Work shop, at bench	70	Midpoint F2.8-F4
Sewing room		
Occasional sewing, coarse thread, large stitches, high contrast—thread-fabric	30	F2
Prolonged sewing, light to medium fabrics	100	F4
Dark fabrics, fine detail, low contrast	200	F5.6
Family room, study room		
Reading, writing		
Books, magazines, newspapers	30	F2
Handwriting, poor copy, reproductions, small type	70	Midpoint F2.8-F4
Study desks	70	Midpoint F2.8-F4
Reading music scores		
Simple scores	30	F2
Advanced scores	70	Midpoint F2.8-F4
Substandard notations	150	Midpoint F4-F5.6
Table games	30	F2

2. Elements of Design

Color, Texture, and Pattern

The interior walls of our homes or apartments make up a large area and create perhaps the greatest amount of emotional response, well-being, and ambiance in our "human environment." As the area and space in our dwellings grow smaller and more compact, and production-line efficiency provides bare rooms without much architectural interest, we rely more and more upon illusions to make our habitat more than just livable, but beautiful.

We are fortunate to have at our disposal thousands of possible wall coverings from which to choose in order to create an interior more to our liking. Added to these are wall decorations, from paintings and prints to decorative shelves and wall-systems on which to display our own precious collections an memorabilia, wallhangings and tapestries, and other accessories.

With all this abundance available, and most of it relatively inexpensive and installable by your own weekend handyman or yourself—the main problem is how to make a choice!

The first thing that has to be done is to analyze the problem. You have probably formed your own sort of lifestyle or have some idea of what you would like that lifestyle to be. You may have color preferences and a feeling for natural textures as opposed to sleek chrome and glass, or perhaps you feel more comfortable surrounded by traditional Colonial or French Provincial furnishings and wall treatments. Whether you are a swinging single, a young couple just starting out, a large family with children, or a couple whose family has been raised and can now finally settle down to a relaxed pace—there are certain factors and design principles which can help you create your own comfortable, personal environment.

While you consider the various wall coverings and decoration available from which to choose, certain basic characteristics or factors will make themselves evident.

These basic design factors are *Color, Texture,* and *Pattern,* and finally *Balance* is necessary to put it all together.

COLOR

Color is the quickest, easiest, and cheapest way to change your surroundings and has the greatest power to change moods and create illusions. Most people prefer one color or combination of colors. Some color schemes are characteristic of certain periods of decoration.

Before we go any further in our discussion of color, it would be best to define some terms that deal with the properties of color. *Hue* refers to the name of the color, such as red or blue. The *Value* of a color is a measure of whether a color is light or dark. A *Tint* is a light or high value of a color (on a vertical scale of white at the top ranging down through different gradations to black at the bottom) and a *Shade* is a dark or low value of a color. The *Intensity* of a color refers to the color's purity, that is the degree of brightness or dullness of that particular color. By adding gray to any color, you lower its intensity and it becomes duller. *Neutral* colors are black, white, and gray, all metallics, and also tints and shades of colors that are predominantly gray or brown in cast, such as beige. *Warm* colors, associated with fire and the sun, are red, yellow, and orange. *Cool* colors are blue, green, and purple or violet, the colors of the sea and sky.

People differ in their color likes and dislikes, and the people using your space must be taken into account. Children, as infants, see only bright colors at first and through their early years prefer light, bright warm colors. Adults, in general, prefer the subtler hues.

The study of the psychology of color gives us more clues as to why we like or dislike certain colors and also an insight into some illusions created by different colors. Color evokes emotion and certain colors have definite appeal to certain personalities.

		Have these qualities:	Are preferred by people who are:
Warm Colors	Red Orange Yellow	Busy Happy Bright Stimulating Cheerful	Emotional Vigorous Extroverted More Social Active
Cool Colors	Green Blue Violet	Relaxing Soft Depressing Sad Quiet	Introverted More interested in self than in the world Passive Solemn

And then there is the symbolism of color—certain colors bring to mind certain things. Here are some examples of color symbolism:

White—Innocence, joy, purity, glory, winter, neutral

Red—Fire, blood, passion, danger, Christmas, Valentine's Day

Yellow—Alertness, intellectual, joyous, cowardice, summer

Blue—Sedation, conservative, calm, cold, remote, pure, ice

Green—Nature cool, fresh, St. Patrick's Day, tranquility, spring

Purple—Royalty, melancholoy, sophistication, Easter

Orange—Friendly, Thanksgiving and Halloween, autumn

Color can create optical illusions. The proper use of color can create the illusion of architectural changes, alter the apparent sun-exposure of a room, and establish the emotional mood of a setting. There are some basic rules of color illusion which are good problem solvers.

Warm colors (red, orange, and yellow) appear to advance toward the viewer visually, tending to make objects look larger and rooms smaller. Warm colors *look* warm, are stimulating and cheerful, and create intimate room settings. Cool colors (blue, green, and violet) visually recede or back off from the viewer. They look cool and restful, and make rooms seem larger and more spacious.

Bright colors of high intensity appear to expand due to their eye-catching purity. They can exaggerate the size of objects and cause areas to close in visually. They are gay and exciting, but can be distracting and unrestful when used in excess.

If you have a long, narrow room, the use of bright, warm colors on the end walls and white on the long side walls will tend to equalize things. If you have a room that is large and barn-like, then the walls in a darker tone of a warm color will make it seem smaller and more friendly.

If you like the sleek sophistication of chrome and glass, consider this dynamic wall mural of Art Deco geometry in silver, black, and burgundy. It's certain to add drama to your dining area! (Environmental Graphics; photo courtesy of Wallcovering Industry Bureau).

Rattan matting, applied to the wall with bamboo strips, is a warm, natural, sound-absorbent material that evokes a South Sea Island feeling, as does the beaded curtain serving as drapery. The bright red-orange porcelain-enamel-finished, free-standing fireplace is a simple and classic design (Majestic Fireplaces).

The charm of a Toile wallpaper, accented by woodwork painted in a contrasting color, serves as introduction to the country Provincial decor throughout the home (York Wall Paper Co.).

A long corridor can be shortened visually by painting the end walls a bright, warm color. In a bright, sunny room, lavender or blue work beautifully. In a darker room with a northern exposure, these same colors turn gray and depressing. The sunny feeling of lots of yellow and white and other bright colors lift the spirits in a room that receives little natural sunlight.

Light colors expand because they reflect light and objects seem larger, yet lighter in weight. They make rooms seem more spacious, are cheerful, and uplifting.

Dark colors contract because they absorb light.

They make objects appear smaller and heavier in weight. Dark colors look warmer and actually are warmer, since they absorb light. Dark colors used in excess can be depressing.

The effect of light and dark colors is particularly apparent in the selection of ceiling and floor colors. The use of a black ceiling in a room with white walls and white carpeting will certainly appear top-heavy! On the other hand, if you have a very high ceiling, the use of a darker shade of the wall color, for instance, will give it a lower, cozier feeling.

The old rigid rules of color combinations and color matching are now disregarded, but the Color Wheel in this section, based on the order in which colors appear when light is refracted through a prism, is still a valuable tool in visualizing color relationships. Red, blue, and yellow, the Primary colors, are equidistant around the circumference of the color wheel. By mixing equal amounts of one primary color with another, the Secondary colors of orange, purple (or violet), and green result. (For example, red and blue make purple, red and yellow make orange, and blue and yellow make green.) The other spaces on the wheel are filled by the Tertiary colors, which are equal combinations of adjacent colors. These are red-violet, red-orange, yellow-orange, yellow-green, blue-green, and blue-violet. The Color Wheel can be quite helpful, as it indicates what colors go well with each other to produce harmonious and pleasing color schemes. Another good rule of thumb concerning the proportion of different colors used in a successful color scheme is to select a basic color to cover about 60 percent of the area of the room. This will be the dominant color in the room and of course create the greatest impact. Choose a second color in a contrasting shade for a bold look, or a coordinated color for a subdued effect. A third color should be used for accents only . . . about 5 percent of the area.

Color Schemes

Monochromatic, analogous, complementary, split-complementary, analogous-complementary, and triadic are technical terms that describe combinations taken from the Color Wheel. But color schemes are merely guideposts. After you have learned the rules, you can stretch or break them. Following are the major color schemes.

The Neutrals. One or two colors with black, white, beige or gray, or any of the metallics (silver, gold, copper, etc.), the simplest of all. The walls might be a very pale gray or silver metallic paper, the sofa a medium gray suede, the coffee table glass and chrome, the carpet a black, white and gray tweed. Black floor cushions and a bright orange upholstered chair for accent could complete the scheme.

The Monochromatic Scheme. One in which many values and intensities of a single color are used, simple and attractive. Walls could be a medium shade of apricot with the woodwork and shag carpeting a deeper value, almost a terra cotta. The bedspread could be a quilt with squares ranging in color from pale apricot, to orange and into warm brown. A chair covered in a bright apricot and shutters on the windows matching the terra cotta of the woodwork would add interest. In order to relieve possible monotony, the use of black and white accents and a varia-

tion of textures are helpful.

The Analogous Scheme. Uses colors which adjoin each other on the Color Wheel, such as yellow, yellow-green, and green; or, red, red-orange, and orange. These colors usually are not in their pure form, rather in varying values and intensities. Usually one of the colors predominates, using the 60 percent, 35 percent, and 5 percent ratio for areas covered.

Analogous Scheme with Complementary Accent. An analogous scheme accented by a color that is opposite on the Color Wheel. For example, a yellow-green, green, and blue-green color scheme with accents of red.

Complementary Scheme. In its basic form, two colors opposite each other on the Color Wheel, such as blue-green and red-orange. Each color makes the other look more attractive and mixed together they make a neutral gray, which indicates a perfect balance. (In vision, green is the after-image of red, the brightest primary color . . . operating rooms and the robes of the doctors and nurses are green in order to minimize eye fatigue.) In this scheme the proportions of the different hues, in various values and intensities, is important.

Near, or Split Complements. A split complementary scheme takes the form of a Y on the Color Wheel, the one arm of the Y pointing, for instance, to yellow-orange, the other to red-orange and the stem to blue.

Double-split Complement. Takes the form of an X on the Color Wheel. For example, the top legs point to yellow-orange and red-orange and the bottom legs to blue-green and blue-violet.

Triad. An excellent color scheme which mixes the three colors located at the points of a triangle placed over the Color Wheel, such as red, blue, and yellow. It offers a wide range of hues, values, and intensities, such as muted tones for the traditional look and vibrant colors with white for a more modern effect.

White, of course, is the lightest of the neutrals and the color most universally relied upon to accent, punctuate, or relieve a color scheme. Next to white and the neutrals, the simplest color scheme to handle and the most successful is the Monochromatic, darkened by black or dark neutrals, lightened by white or pale neutrals, and varied by textures and patterns.

One of the recent developments in color popularity has been the OP colors. OP colors are used to create optical illusions or effects, causing movements of the eye. OP colors are strong primary and secondary colors of the spectrum, such as red, blue, orange, and purple juxtaposed in clashing combinations with the visual effect of seeming to move. For slow movements the spectrum colors in their rainbow order or complementary colors are used. For fast movements, dissonant colors are used.

Along with the OP colors come free designs or

Supergraphics that move from wall to wall and from floor to ceiling. These designs direct the eye around the room, hide architectural deformities from view, create headboards or other interests where there were none before, and can be a fascinating new method of creating an individual living space from modern cubicles.

With the ecological movement has come an interest in the Naturals. These are colors taken from nature such as earth and sky tones, the various shades of green found in a forest, the tawny golds and oranges and browns achieved from natural dyes, the beiges, off-whites, and grays of natural wool, the cool blues and greens of water—to create a peaceful, comfortable and yes, natural environment.

Some people wish to reconstruct totally or in part the period of history in which they would prefer to live. Authentic color lines are created by paint, wallpaper, and fabric companies for adaptation to our sterile interiors. They are well researched and presented. Williamsburg Green and Sutter's Gold, Early American Turkey Red, Chinese lacquer Red, French Blue and so on are classic colors that have stood the test of time and are always pleasing.

If you have a beautiful collection of blue and white Chinese porcelains, brown and white Bennington ware, a favorite painting or print, a great colorful fabric, an interesting area rug or wall-hanging, a striking wallpaper, use them to create a successfully personal color scheme for your room.

Color balance must be achieved by carefully selecting areas and volumes that are to be light, dark, pale, or intense in color. Colors should never be strewn around wholesale, they cancel each other out. A needless contrast, such as a black ceiling and walls with a white carpet on the floor, is unnatural and annoying to the eye. Always consider where you want attention to be focused—on a seating area, a particular painting or piece of furniture, or a fireplace—and then call on color to pull it off.

So far we have only spoken of one room at a time. Color coordination and harmony should be considered for the house or apartment as a whole design entity. This does not mean that each room should follow the same color scheme, but that each room in the whole should emphasize one color, perhaps from the general overall color scheme so that as you move from space to space, the color flows harmoniously to create a pleasing and consistent environment.

Practical Hints

In making decisions on color, it is important to keep in mind the fact that the finished job will look darker than the sample, particularly if paint is being used on a large area.

Look at color samples in the same light as the conditions under which they will be used—natural light for exterior, filament or fluorescent lighting for interior.

The size of the area in many cases will affect the values of color. Wall areas that reflect each other will intensify and purify each other's color, tending to removal of gray tones.

When you check color samples against other colors in a room, remember also to check against the colors which will be visible when the doors to adjoining areas are standing open. Smooth color transitions from room to room are important in achieving complete color harmony.

TEXTURE

Texture has recently been recognized as an important and powerful element in the design of the contemporary interior. The successful handling of texture as a design element can and does make the modern home or apartment more suited to everyday comfort and modern living, and more beautiful.

A number of new developments have contributed to a renewed interest in texture in our lives. We have more time for recreation and just plain enjoyment of leisure. Along with this have come the new comfortable knitted fabrics for clothing and upholstery, and the new synthetic copies of expensive sensuous materials such as suede and other leathers, velvets, silks, satins, and the gorgeous metallics. With the emphasis on preserving our natural materials has come a renewed appreciation of the warm luster of wood, and the possibility of achieving the same effect without chopping down all our forests.

Texture, the nature of a material, refers to the three-dimensionality and surface characteristics of a given material. Texture, as the description of the surface aspect, may be shiny or dull, rough or smooth, hard or soft, scratchy or soothing, rigid or pliable, luxurious or rugged, light and filmy or heavy and sturdy, transparent or opaque and so on. Texture as the description of the surface aspect of a material may include:

1. material in its natural state;
2. processed or finished materials;
3. woven fabrics or other materials;
4. applied decoration, such as raised pattern or carving or molded design;
5. synthetic materials manufactured to duplicate as faithfully as possible the original material;
6. graphic representation of a material, such as a photograph or drawing.

A cozy conversational corner in a living room with international flavor, this room setting contains an interesting combination of textures, such as the white-washed brick wall and the plain, painted one as a background for a fascinating collection of pillows, rush covered bottles, appliqued Mexican molas framed on the wall, and potted palm (Hedrich-Blessing Photo).

A judicious use of redwood paneling in this contemporary living room sheathes the fireplace and chimney; it is also placed strategically as beams. Its warmth contrasts with the walls, painted white, and the black iron spiral staircase and the quarry tile floor, creating a light and airily spacious living space (California Redwood Association).

Redwood paneling adds warmth and a country feeling to this contemporary dining room. The classic design of the glass and chrome table and the cane and chrome chairs, plus the slim metal blinds at the windows, contrast with the natural wood (California Redwood Association).

In order to better understand the importance of texture in our lives, we should perhaps discuss briefly how texture is perceived. Texture is primarily perceived through feeling, the tactile sense. The most powerful perception of the texture of a material comes from the actual feeling of it . . . the pleasure of feeling material with the fingers. Texture can also be perceived through seeing. The rough or smooth quality of a material may be seen and its texture conjured through previous experience with that material. Because we have felt things before and are familiar with the aspects of certain materials, we associate materials with certain qualities.

Texture is a strong element in the design of interiors and in the illusions it is capable of creating because of the association which feeling and looking at a material bring to mind. Different moods may be created in a room by the selection and arrangement of the various materials.

Texture in Wall Coverings

Perhaps a listing of some of the textures available to us today as wall coverings, along with their special characteristics, will provide us with a resource stockpile from which to more successfully create our own individual and comfortable surroundings.

Wood Paneling. Warm, natural, rich, secure, and strong, easily cared for, depending upon the kind of wood (i.e., birch, walnut, rosewood) and the type of finish (natural, weathered, oil finish, highly polished); an extremely versatile material.

Brick. Warm, natural, durable, rugged, depending on the color of brick and method of laying it, many different effects can be achieved. Brick may be painted or whitewashed for a country look, left natural to bring warmth to plain interior and even glazed in bright colors for a very sleek look.

Cork. Warm, natural, absorbs sound, has a rich look and feel.

Fabric. Soft, warm absorbs sound well, depending upon the fabric has many different characteristics: burlap—rough, rugged, sturdy, earthy, durable, informal; felt and wool—warm, soft, absorbs sound; cotton—crisp, good colors and prints; brocade—rich, traditional, luxurious. Manner in which fabric is applied to wall can affect textural appearance. Fabric can be stretched and applied flat, or shirred on a rod or pleated, or can even turn a room into a tent!

Stone. Feeling of rough warmth and rugged outdoor quality, durability and good solid stability, heavy texture.

Mirrors or Mirror Tiles. Reflective, cool, shiny, sleek, sophisticated, capable of creating illusion of additional space.

Carpeting, Carpet Tiles and Wall Tapestries. Soft,

Brick not only adds an outdoor, casual touch when used with this metal fireplace, but gives an extra measure of fireproofing as well (Malm Fireplaces, Inc.).

This bath, with a sunken tub enclosed by a private Oriental garden, combines ceramic mosaic with a stone wall, slate stepping stones, and smooth pebbles for a consistently appealing earth-toned set of textures (American Olean Tile Co.).

The "enchanted forest" in this wall mural creates a grand romantic illusion for this contemporary remodeled dining room. The winter wildwood of black, beige, and olive against silvery mylar background, along with the mirrored walls, results in the sparkling illusion of endless space (The Jack Denst Designs, Inc.).

Full storage walls combine beauty with usefulness in this Colonial living room. Here wall-to-wall stock panel doors of ponderosa pine were used to duplicate the richness of custom-made sculptured paneling, but at less expense. One door was cut in half to produce the decorative panel over the fireplace. Then the whole paneled wall was painted an accent color, as was the window frame. With the ceiling beams, moldings, and the Grandfather clock and print grouping, a unity of period and style was achieved (National Woodwork Manufacturers Assn.).

Wood and stone go together inside your house just as well as they do in nature. Wood beams enhance the warm, woodsy effect (Western Woods Products Association).

The interesting architecture of this bath makes it a unique showplace of textures...redwood ceiling and paneling and a beautiful ceramic tile mural in the bathtub alcove inspired by the graceful branches of a willow tree. The rough, natural stone plus an interesting mirror installation over the counter, frames the corner to lengthen the room and create the impression of looking outdoors (American Olean Tile Company).

warm, luxurious, absorbs sound, "feelable" texture, cozy.

Wood (or Plastic) Molding, Batten, Lattice, Strips, Beams. Can be used to simulate architectural features such as traditional wall paneling, chair rails, exposed roof beams, the outdoor feeling of lattice, and more.

Stucco or Textured Paint. Rough country feeling, absorbs sound, gives depth, adds warmth; good combined with heavy wood beams for traditional, sturdy, natural look.

Ceramic Tile. Very versatile material, can be sleek, shining and sophisticated, with matt finish has modern natural feeling, very country and warm in the form of hand-made Mexican tile.

Rush Squares, Tatami Mats, Woven Straw Lahala Mats, and Bamboo Fencing. Soft, natural, sound absorbant, bamboo shiny and smooth; exotic Oriental feeling.

Marble. Sleek, cool, shining, sophisticated, hard, and reflective.

Metal. Tiles, strips or panels—cool, shiny, hard, reflective—stainless steel sophisticated and copper more country in feeling. Also foil paper either plain or with design printed over—very reflective and sophisticated.

Formica and Other Plastic Laminates. Hard material can be made with shiny smooth or matt suede-like finish, also imitates slate and leather, etc., in embossed texture.

Grasscloth. Made by gluing woven native grasses from Japan onto paper backing, extremely luxurious natural texture, Oriental feeling.

Shiki. Oriental shantung silk glued to a paper background, lustrous and elegant, with the characteristic silk texture.

Flocked Wallpaper. Included in here because its texture imitates cut velvet, is warm and luxurious.

Leather. Used in tile form or applied like fabric to walls, sometimes tooled or tufted. Recent use of suede on walls very soft and sensuous. Thought to be masculine and mellow.

It would be almost impossible to include and analyze all possible textures that can be used as wall coverings. New ways of applying different materials and new methods synthetically imitating natural materials are being developed all the time.

In general, we can say that smooth, shiny textures tend to recede and reflect light and sound, whereas rough, dull textures tend to advance and absorb light and sound. Textures such as wood, brick, stucco, and stone, usually appeal to us as natural, homey, and countryish traditional walls. In contrast, mirrored walls, metallic wallpapers, shiny plastic wall covering, glass, chrome and stainless steel seem more modern and sophisticated, less personal.

It is usually best not to mix too many different tex-

An analogous color scheme (above) using yellows and oranges is reinforced by the matching tablecloth and shades (Hercules, Inc.).

Natural wood paneling (left) that continues on through the soaring window wall to form the exterior wall and deck, plus the natural earth tones of the Navaho rug, set the color scheme for this contemporary home (Western Wood Products).

This supergraphic (below) draws attention from the hall toward the seating area; the earth tones add warmth to an otherwise plain, undefined area (Wood Davies & Co., Ltd.).

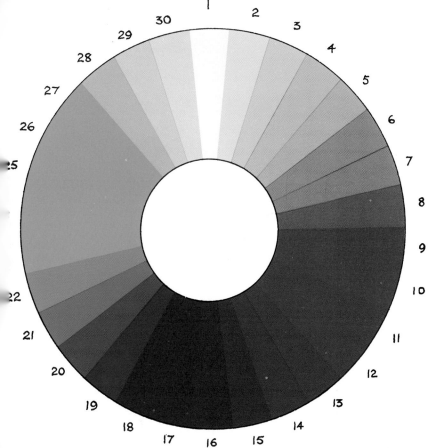

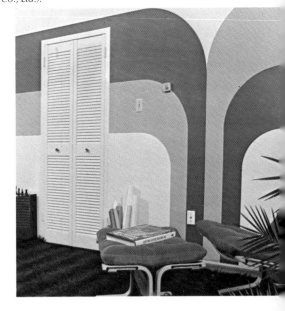

Color wheel from the Oxford Companion to Art; edited by Harold Osborn, 1970, reproduced by permission of the Oxford University Press, London.

The openness of this cathedral ceiling enables us to view how the basic complementary color scheme of blue and orange is carried throughout the house. The quarry tile floor and chair cushions pick up the orange tones of the warm beige grasscloth. The living and dining room have blue as their main theme, and both blue and orange are combined in the balcony sitting room. The dark wood beams create a pattern of their own against the white walls and ceilings, and emphasize the home's spaciousness (Hedrich-Blessing photo).

Open-planning to make best use of available space in this apartment necessitates a blending and coordinating of colors, textures, and patterns. With a dominant color of orange, used with woodtones, this wall covering has a design that can almost be considered a texture in itself (Formica).

Pale-blue steel cabinets below, wood ones above, have a clean flush-door design and combine well with an assortment of natural wall coverings. Ceramic tiles are used behind the countertop grill, and the other walls in the inner core of the kitchen are natural fieldstone. Remaining walls are woodpanelled, as is the hood over the grill (Saint Charles' Kitchens).

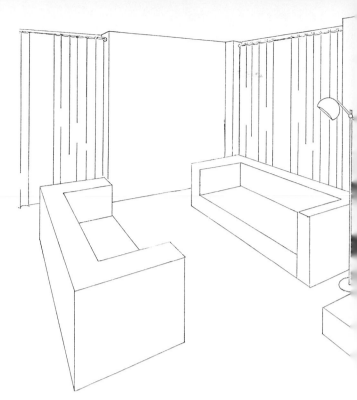

For an easy and inexpensive way to experiment with creating your own color scheme and personal environment, make a quick sketch on paper of some part of the room or rooms you are planning. It need not be in perspective, but it will help you visualize if you make some attempt at drawing things in proportion. Then take the basic drawing and color it in with colored markers or pencils or crayons, approximating as closely as possible the hues and values of the colors you are thinking of using. Even though it will not look professional, you will be amazed at the different effects you can create, and at what you learn about color, texture and balance while making the sketch.

Here, we have taken the focal corner of a living room, showing the two windows and a conversational grouping, and made a basic sketch of big color areas—not including end tables, table lamps etc.—just concentrating on the basic large shapes of sofas, draperies and other important color components. We have then proceeded to decorate the same room in four different schemes.

(Above left) This silk-screened photographic mural provides the perfect backdrop for an informal dining area (Environmental Graphics, photo courtesy of Lis King).

(Center left) This family dining room in the modified Georgian "Secretary House" of Exeter, New Hampshire, was built in 1750 by John Giddings. It later became the home of Joseph Pearson (Secretary of State for New Hampshire in the early 1800's), and is now furnished just as it was during his lifetime. The dining room, with sliding shutters, woodwork, and dado painted a soft, grayed green, and upper walls white, contains an interesting combination of Queen Anne and Chippendale furniture (reproduced courtesy of Henry Ford Museum from the Collections of Greenfield Village, Dearborn, Mich.).

(Below left) A forerunner of today's one-room efficiency apartment, this room reflects the stark simplicity of home life in early New England. Nevertheless, the natural wood and brick lend a warmth that is well reproduced in today's wall coverings. This is the "Plympton House," of Massachusetts (reproduced courtesy of Henry Ford Museum from the Collections of Greenfield Village, Dearborn, Mich.).

Blue-green and yellow-green combine with the warm tones of natural brick to create this cozy room with an Early American feeling. Notice how the checked wall covering and the shuttered window treatment contribute to this style. Even though receding colors were used, the textures and the use of natural brick on the fireplace wall plus the antique weathervane mounted over the fireplace, create a homey atmosphere.

And now a soft, luxurious, yet highly sophisticated setting in neutral tones of gray and beige. The interest here is created by the texture (corduroy) of the sofas, carpeting (plush and deep), the pattern of the wallpapered wall (really more of a texture than a patterned paper), and the draperies of a heavily twisted fabric (such as raw silk). There is a touch of silver mylar in the wallpaper, along with an accent of orange, and the dark gray walls are painted in a matt finish. Sleek tables of chrome and glass would fit into this decorating style.

Bright touches of color and a white-tiled floor give a light and airy space. An outdoor feeling is achieved using many plants and a color scheme of white, bright green, and pale yellow. The two green sofas and the area rug with the vivid Mexican colors make up the big interest area. White wooden slat blinds for the windows go well with the wall by the fireplace grouping, which has wood paneling installed horizontally and is painted white; the white serves as an excellent background for the macramé piece and green sofas.

This room, with its complementary color scheme of orange and blue, has been planned with the young family in mind. The walls have been covered in natural beige burlap (good sound-conditioning as well as good looks). A simulated, vinyl fabric wall covering would be even more suitable for small children. The shelves can be adjusted to hold books, puzzles, records, games, objects made by children, etc. Curtains are easy-going cafés on rings. A rugged, faded blue for the sofas, the denim stripe on the ottoman, and brightly colored carpet of tough tweed, give wear-resistance and easy care.

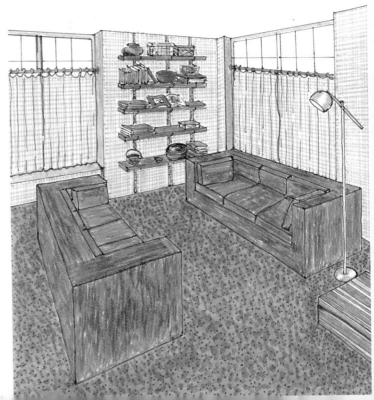

The spirit of the French countryside in this charming dining room is carried out with hardboard paneling that is a handsome reproduction of wall treatments found in French provincial homes of the 18th century. The white paneling is also used as a facing on the bifold doors that turn one complete wall into a concealed storage area. The fresh blue and green in the drapery print, carpet, chair seats, and table cloth, combine with the white paneling to show off the collection of china on the wall (Masonite Corp., Paul Krauss AID).

Just the place for a sunny breakfast! The floral-and-fruit striped provincial pattern combine to bring out the dark beams and show off the home owner's basket collection (York Wall Paper Co.).

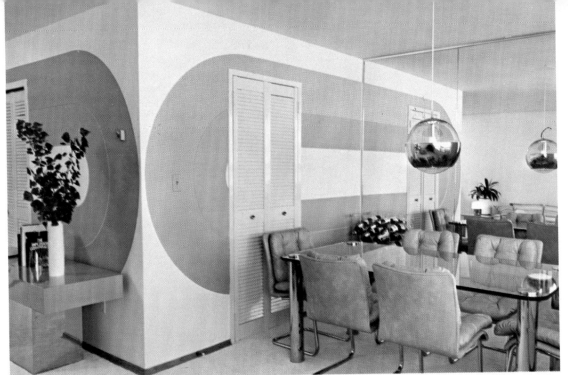

The transition and movement of colors in this painted Supergraphic add excitement to the plain space. Notice how the mirrored wall completes the graphic design and adds another dimension to the room (Wood Davies & Co., Ltd.).

Use of a bright, large-scale mural is effective in this small living room, primarily through the colors selected. The brilliant silk-screened design takes adjacent warm and cool colors in teardrop and circle forms and places them against a white vinyl ground. The design advances and recedes, and background and white sofas fade into one. The flanged wall of tiny mirrors reflects the scene in a colorful, reflective mosaic (Jack Denst Designs, Inc.).

Sleek glass, bright red, and shimmering gold mylar highlight a sophisticated conversation corner. Note the lighting in the cabinet, making the collection another decorative feature (Jack Denst Designs, Inc.).

White hexagon-shaped ceramic tile has been used on the backsplash and grille facing in this kitchen as a dramatic contrast to the wood paneling of the cabinets and other wall and ceiling surfaces. These natural materials have been repeated in the floor, which is the same hexagon tile installed in a grid of teak wood. This combination of easy maintenance and dramatic use of contrasting textures results in an extremely effective, livable kitchen design (American Olean Tile Co.).

This colorful, highly efficient kitchen is built on a corridor arrangement. The breakfast room is seen through the archway, with its bright yellow and white and green daffodil wall covering. Yellow tile lines the archway entering the breakfast room and the alcove. The white stucco kitchen wall adds a rougher texture to the room (American Olean Tile Co.).

This kitchen brings the outdoors in, using natural fieldstone old barn siding, a brick floor, and a wood cathedral ceiling with wood cabinets (Wood-Mode photo).

This Supergraphic creates interest and focusses on the living room area in a one-room apartment. The light, bright colors and the design draw your eye right to the balcony (Wood Davies & Co., Ltd.).

A heavily textured fabric-backed vinyl wall covering in this earth-toned setting gives additional sense of space and three-dimensionality. The window treatment uses the same wall covering (Stauffer Chemical Co.).

A deep, rich, parquetlike design of hardboard wall paneling has been applied to the seating wall, a handsome divider screen, and also to the ceiling treatment between the beams to effect a Mediterranean feeling in this comfortable living room. A rough plaster look, achieved with prefinished hardboard panel siding, is used to construct the seating platform and also creates a floor-to-ceiling fireplace wall. Ceramic tile on the floor is in keeping with the feeling of the room (Masonite Corp.).

It is hard to believe that this glamorous bath (above left) was created with the use of fabric-backed, scrubbable, strippable, prepasted wall covering. The two coordinated patterns form an interesting contrast; the foil background reflects the light, and together with the white flooring the whole bath space almost seems to float (Stauffer Chemical Co.)

Here is an example (above) of coordinated wall coverings that relate adjoining rooms to each other. A stripe printed on a textured background of fabric-backed vinyl wall covering accents the window wall of the bedroom, covers the cornice board over the windows, and is repeated on the walls of the adjoining bath. The remaining walls of the bedroom are covered with the plain off-white linenlike textured background of the stripe. Note how the vertical stripes increase the apparent height of the walls and the cornice board over the window increases its size (Stauffer Chemical Co.).

A handsome tailored plaid (left) in gray and copper, this prepasted strippable fabric-backed vinyl wall covering not only goes on easily, but also comes down when you're ready for a change! The colors and pattern give this bath more of a dressing room feeling (Stauffer Chemical Co.).

The serenity of this Japanese-influenced bathroom design is due both to the proportions of the architecture and to the pure textures of bamboo, quarry tile, and natural wood. The tub wall is covered with panels of laminated plastic in a marble pattern (Kohler).

Furniture, wall covering, quilt, and accessories all coordinate to achieve a quaint, oldfashioned setting (York Wall Paper Co.).

Sophisticated excitement from a textured fabric-backed wall covering that simulates bamboo blinds. The same pattern has been used to cover the tailored window shades. The analogous color scheme—orange, red-orange, and red—is cheerful and stimulating (Stauffer Chemical Co.).

A real space-maker patterned wall covering was used in this dining area. The Art Deco design is a fabric-backed, prepasted, scrubbable, strippable vinyl that goes particularly well with the cane chairs and sleek accessories (Stauffer Chemical Company).

Close-up of a matching provincial print wallpaper and fabric. The use of a small pattern, all over the room, creates the illusion that the room is larger (York Wall Paper Co.).

This mural paper, "Scenic America" printed by Zuber & Co., in Rixheim Alsace in 1834, is mounted in the diplomatic Reception Room of the White House. The historic paper contains several views of American natural wonders. The portion shown here is of the West Point landscape (left), and the port of Boston (right). (Copyright by White House Historical Association; photograph by the National Geographic Society.)

An accent panel of Western Wood board paneling sets off a modern version of the fireplace in this living room that is open on three sides (Western Wood Products).

The small provincial floral stripes add intimacy to this sitting room, with its mantel accented in gold. The more formal and airy crewel-like floral pattern in the dining room coordinates with the sitting room pattern (York Wall Paper Co.).

The deep orange-painted walls of this large bedroom and adjoining bath set off the white-painted furniture and shag rug to show the warmth possible but often not found in a bedroom (The Carpet and Rug Institute).

This beautiful vinyl wall covering combines silver foil and white flocking in a light bamboo design. The reflective quality of the foil enlarges the apparent size and brightness of this small, rather dark dining area. The sleek, shininess of the foil balances the rich texture of the flocking (Columbus Coated Fabrics).

The dramatic effect of this entrance comes from exploiting the home's two-story design. The entrance is at the top, with the openness of the descent to the living room accented by a gallery wall spanning both floors. Dark-stained stair treads cantilevered from the walls stand out against the golden coloring of western hemlock tongue-and-groove paneling (Western Wood Products; Edgar Wilson Smith, IAI, Portland, Oregon).

A relaxing vacation home with the warmth of natural wood accented by the striking black metal hood of the fireplace. The carpeting forms the sunken conversation pit with built-in seating (California Redwood Assn.).

A crisp Early American welcome! This entrance hall is fortunate in having a beautiful classical wooden doorway with fanlight above. The woodwork has been painted white to stand out against the medallion wallpaper. The stairs and railing have been painted the same gold that appears in the paper, so that this area is accented without competing with the door frame (York Wall Paper Co.).

tures in one area or any illusion or accent will be lost. A good rule is to mix a fine texture with a medium one, or a rough texture with a medium one and not make the contrast too great. On the other hand, using all fine textures or all rough ones cancels out their individual effects.

Another factor to be considered is suitability and compatibility of textures. We have discussed the qualities of the various textures and with these in mind, can consider carefully the effect you are trying to achieve and how best to reach it. Don't mix metaphors, so to speak, and place mirror squares surrounding a massive, rough fieldstone fireplace.

Totally Individual Environments

Many people are experimenting with new materials for interiors and new uses for new materials. Industrial foam, for instance, which until recently has been used primarily as an insulation material, can cover old cracked walls or recontour areas by creating cave-like abstract shapes. The foam covers a plywood and wire understructure that roughly approximates the intended shape for perhaps a seating alcove.

Using only minimal furniture and no wall decoration, Aleksandra Kasuba, a New York artist, has been creating stretch fabric environments. The nylon knit fabric is stretched from floor to ceiling in a definite pattern creating a maze of tunnels, open walks, small and large places, with ramps and pillows. The fabric is translucent so that one is surrounded by soft, glowing light.

Along with the trend toward smaller living spaces, we find more wall-systems containing not only shelf, cabinet and drawer storage, but fold-away beds and dining tables. At the same time, seating seems to be more and more pillow-like and is arranged in the center of the room.

All this illustrates innovative and experimental ways in which some people strive for an individual environment in increasingly crowded living spaces without much character or personality.

PATTERN

There remains one more tool at our disposal to help us individualize and beautify our interior surroundings . . . and that is Pattern. We are talking here about pattern as a design on cloth or paper. Let us not forget, however, that pattern is created by the texture, color, and form in a room, as well as by conventional design. Pattern exists in the grain of wood and the contour of the furniture, in the mosaic of a tiled wall—all the elements of a room.

Pattern creates interest and spice in our interiors. It stops the eye and draws attention to the area in which it is placed. Large patterns shrink the apparent size of a room and small patterns make the room appear larger. A room covered with matching wallpaper and fabric for the draperies can appear to increase the size of the room.

A room without pattern can be monotonous, yet too much pattern can make one restless. Many rules have been laid down on the proportion of pattern to be used, such as one quarter to one third of the room area, but the important thing is to achieve a pleasing (to you) balance between color, texture, and pattern. The total design of a room consists of an interplay of color, pattern and texture. All these elements together create a kind of rhythm, dependent on all its parts being in balance.

Patterned Wall Covering

In the context of wall covering, there are many different types of patterns. Many have been discussed in Section One. Of these patterns, certain ones can be used to achieve particular effects.

Geometrics. Based on angles and curves, this type of pattern is probably the most powerful illusion-creator of all. Geometrics are concerned with line, and it is the different types of line that create effects.

Vertical lines generate excitement and upward movement and can be used to add height to an area. They also convey the dignity and pomp. Stripes and vertical lines predominate in classical styles, and are very good in reception rooms and entrance halls.

Horizontal lines give a feeling of rest and repose, relaxation and comfort. The eye is drawn from side to side, giving the illusion of width.

Diagonal lines create movement in their direction and give depth and three-dimensionality. They are very powerful in potential to attract the eye . . . very restless in their movement.

Curving lines in a pattern serve as transition between horizontal and vertical. The movement of curving lines is very pleasing to the eye and can give a feeling of well-being and comfort. The sinuous curving lines found in 18th-century furniture is coming back in figure-hugging, pillow-shaped sofas and chairs today, thus giving us a comfort lacking in modernistic interiors. The very great value of Geometric patterns is their ability to combine pleasingly with florals and other patterns. You have to be careful to balance the scale (generally large with smaller, and bold with less bold for contrast). The colors must have a common base, say one common color appearing in all the various patterns. These patterns are very useful for uniting a series of rooms or areas in a house or apartment. Geometrics are also useful for covering cracked or defective walls and architectural irregularities.

The random width, vertical stripes of this fascinating wall covering create, along with the low furniture, a startling effect of ceiling height in a standard apartment. The shag carpet, plants, and soft fabric covering the seating and tables counterbalance the stark quality of the wallcovering. No further wall decoration is necessary since the random width stripes seem to undulate and create enough interest on their own (Wallcovering Industry Bureau).

Small areas can be given a feeling of greater spaciousness by installing paneling horizontally instead of vertically. The low, soft and cushiony seating, the plush carpet, and the warmth of the woodgrained paneling, create an area of restful comfort (Marlite Paneling).

Panels, Scenics, and Murals. They can visually push walls outward and create any scene and ambiance you wish, from a charming New England harbor, to a formal Versaille garden, the blues and greens of a Caribbean beach, to the strongly forceful Supergraphics.

Borders. Relatively rare these days, which is unfortunate as they are another powerful tool for directing the eye, finishing off a formal room, covering up gaps or rough spots in the walls. They can be used to create panels and other architectural features.

Novelty and Conversation Pieces. These patterns are always with us. They must be dealt with carefully, as one usually rapidly tires of the motif. They are generally offered for kitchen, baths, and children's rooms. The main guide to go by in this category is—is it a good design esthetically? and is it in good taste?

There is one more category—that of a *pattern printed on a texture*. The most popular of these lately is the pattern printed on foil or metallic paper. These may be florals or geometrics, and they are reflective and greatly useful in creating an illusion of space. Patterns printed on cork and burlap and grasscloth textures are also to be found. In general, caution is to be advised in the use of these papers. The texture itself is often enough and stands very well alone.

Stenciling

Stenciling, applying design with paint and brush through cut-out patterns, should be included in the category of wall decoration. It was a method used for decorating walls, floors, and furniture in early America. Simple to do and inexpensive, authentic patterns are available from museums and other sources—or you can make up your own personalized design.

These bold diagonal lines draw the eye around the room, to give an appearance of added size to an otherwise small kitchen (Hotpoint photo).

The curving, dynamic movement is broken up by vertical lines in this abstract wallpaper. The reflection of light on the metallic background, and the discontinuous curves serve both to catch the eye and to set off the relatively heavy mirror and picture frames (Standard Coated Products wallpaper; photo courtesy of the Wallcovering Industry Bureau).

Putting It All
Together

We have just discussed the various design principles involved in the selection of wall coverings (color, texture, pattern, and balance or harmony), and discovered some of the ways in which illusions may be created in order to correct architectural shortcomings and turn your home into a very personalized environment. And in the preceding section a general survey was presented of the various wall coverings available, as well as information on the nature and selection of paintings, prints, and other decorative objects that can enrich the walls of your home or apartment.

Now it is time for us to put all of this knowledge together, and apply it to your own specific situation. After that we shall have to decide how to combine different kinds of wall coverings for optimum effect, and how to display collections, decorative objects, and so on, in an appropriate and attractive manner.

WHERE TO BEGIN?

First you must look at your problem and analyze it. A family conference is necessary to make some basic decisions on color likes and dislikes, and what kind of an interior everyone agrees upon, or rather, what kind of lifestyle they desire. Whether you are single or a member of a group, a great deal of inward looking is needed at this point.

Are you a conservative, home-loving person whose life centers around home and family? Your home should suggest great warmth and comfort...a simple traditional background in earth colors is probably for you. Is yours a gay and social life with lots of people around? Your home should be planned with an eye to entertaining, using bright, light colors expressing a mood of celebration. If

books, conversation, art, and music are your interests, let these be expressed in the way you decorate your home.

Now is the time to talk with your family about the type or style of furniture most of you agree upon or perhaps an eclectic combination of styles. You may require a feeling of restful comfort, or a striking, formal setting for entertaining in the grand style, or most probably for entering more frequently, with "easy-on-the-hostess" casual get-togethers. Perhaps there are some children (and somehow, along with children come dogs, cats, etc!) in the family. Whether they are small children or teenagers, there will be a lot of traffic, and wear and tear on your walls, furniture, and other surfaces. A careful consideration of everyone's needs must be made and wall treatments selected accordingly.

The space that you are planning to decorate must also be carefully analyzed. You must ask yourself, "What is the proposed use of this space...How many people will be using it at one time?...What is the length of time that people will be using this space?...How large is the space and what are its assets and liabilities?...What is the orientation of this space—does it face North or South?...What effect will all this have upon color selection?" and many more questions.

Color schemes

Whether you are planning to decorate one room or the whole house, some sort of general overall color plan must be made. This does not mean that each room will repeat the same color scheme, but that there will be a link in color (the same floor covering perhaps) and a certain continuity of feeling in the furnishings.

If your decision has been in favor of natural materials, such as wood, brick, wool, straw or rattan, stucco, ceramic tile and so on, then your whole house will reflect this feeling, not necessarily with wood-panelled walls, or brick floors, or leather furniture throughout, but with a

84

A truly elegant, but warm, living room. The redwood offers a striking but comfortable setting, and its simplicity acts as a frame and focus to the large painting on the fireplace wall (California Redwood Assocition).

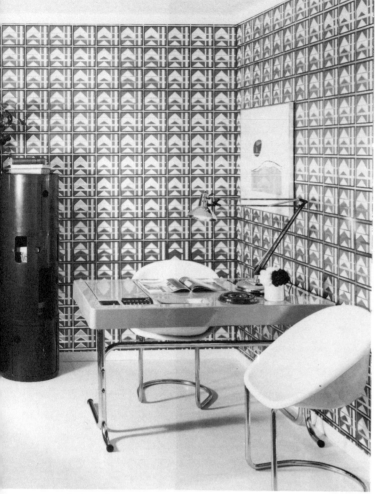

An angular geometric patterned wall covering with a touch of metallic sets off the rounded features of this modernistic furniture grouping, to form a good study or work area (Wall-Tex by Columbus Coated Fabrics).

pleasant balance and interchange between the different natural materials.

Perhaps your family has decided upon a strictly modern, space-age environment, with the use of plastics, mirrors, metal and glass, with a color scheme of white accented by primary colors. It must be said here that no matter what the theme, in order to achieve balance and interest, every scheme must have a contrast between warm and cold materials, soft and hard, dull and shiny. For example, the extravagant use of a textured rug as floor-covering or wall hanging can set off a sleek, modern atmosphere.

If your desire is to live in the manner of our forefathers—the gracious Colonial home, Williamsburg revisited, or a reconstruction of the comfortable

"keeping room" or family-room living around the fireplace used for cooking and warmth in Early American times, then the entire living space can reflect this spirit with Shaker-inspired furniture designs, white walls with a display of old farm tools, fieldstone fireplace, a colorful handmade quilt hung on another wall or used as a bedspread with a brass headboard, and maybe a calico patterned wallpaper in the entrance hall over a white painted woodpaneled dado. Plain painted walls can be stenciled with traditional Early American or Colonial designs, or whatever designs you wish, to add pattern.

We could go on and on in this discussion of different periods and what goes with what successfully. We are, however, committed in this book to discuss wall coverings primarily, in order to help you decide which type of wall covering will meet your needs and achieve the illusions you desire.

Limitations

One of the first problems to be settled is that of budget, of course. In general, paint is your least expensive decorating tool, with wallpaper a close second. Fabric can carry a lot of punch for a little investment, and wood paneling can now be found in many different price ranges. There are also many relatively inexpensive simulations of brick, marble, ceramic tile, and even plastic laminates, that simulate rare and costly woods. In other words, for almost every luxurious decorative material, there is its less costly but effective counterpart.

Another consideration that will affect your choice is whether the wall covering you have selected can be applied by yourself or whether you will have to hire someone else to do it.

If the walls that you will be covering are severely damaged and cracked, they will either have to be repaired or covered with a material such as wood paneling, carpeting, fabric, or some other material which will hide the imperfections. Some patterns and textured or flocked wallpaper are effective for this purpose also. A wallpaper border is another way to hide imperfections particularly between wall and ceiling.

If you are renting a house or apartment, you may find yourself faced with a ruling against nailing or fastening anything directly to the walls, a restriction against wallpaper (only paint allowed) or, in reverse, the requirement of wallpaper on every wall. Do not despair, there are many ways to solve all these problems in an attractive manner—with today's materials, almost any illusion is possible! And strippable wall coverings make it possible for you to easily remove your desired pattern and even take it with you to your next home. Fabric, especially attractive and practical sheets (bedsheets) can be staplegunned to the walls, as can woven rattan matting. A whole plywood framework can be made to cover one whole wall (fastened to real wall with small insignificant nails) and then covered with wood paneling, cork, paper or whatever you wish.

Exteriors

At this point, some mention must be made of the exterior of the house. It is bound to have some influence on how you treat the interior. Suppose your house is a faithful replica or greatly suggestive of a certain period, such as Georgian, English Tudor, Cape Cod, Classic Revival, Midwest Victorian, Southwest adobe, or a Northwest redwood contemporary; while a slavish reproduction of the period in the interior is not necessary, or necessarily desirable, there should be some sort of harmony with or reflection of the exterior.

Now there are, or course, some instances where you have no control over the exterior, such as apartments and condominiums, and the hallways are designed by a builder and decorated by a committee. (This does not include older homes that can be updated with a more contemporary exterior color scheme or more extensive remodeling.) Still, plain modern exteriors can have Early American charm with the addition of a Deacon's bench by the front entrance; or, extremely functional hallway in an apartment building, could have a colorful hand-painted ceramic French Provincial Lavabo hanging by the door, or even just a distinctive Federal eagle doorknocker. In other words, the front door and the exterior of your home are the first introduction to and reflection of your lifestyle. But enough of the exterior, the interior is our main concern.

ENTRANCE AREAS

The easiest way to begin at the beginning is with the entrance hall. After the exterior, this is the real introduction for visitors to you and your family's personality and style of living. In this important role, the entrance hall must get its message across immediately. Since it is generally a fairly small space, and an area in which people do not spend much time, it can be as dramatic and outspoken as you wish! This is not the place for cold, anonymous, strictly functional decorating...here is the opportunity for exuberant originality, even a touch of extrava-

gance. As a place where your guests are welcomed, but do not usually spend much time, overstatement of your personality is not only permissible, but encouraged!

Now that your creative instincts have been aroused, consider your entryway's existing assets, liabilities, and basic architectural elements. Are you fortunate enough to have a graceful spiral staircase reminiscent of those found in gracious Southern mansions; do you have an attractively proportioned cut-glass fanlight over the front door and matching sidelights? Interesting woodwork and architectural features should be highlighted by painting them a different color or lighter or darker than the walls. If the walls are to be papered, and in the large hall you have a spiral staircase, you could have an appropriate historic mural or a large-scale crewel flower design, and then one of the predominant colors in the paper could be used on the woodwork. For example, the woodwork around the interesting doorway could be painted white, the door black, and the walls a bright citron yellow over white-painted woodpaneled wainscoting.

If your home is modern with open steps (stairs without risers) that are in effect transparent and through which you can see into the rest of the house, the color scheme and wall treatment must be compatible with what you can see of the other living areas, creating a harmonious whole.

An entrance hall should ideally include a closet in which to hang up visitor's wraps, and perhaps a bench or chair on which to sit or some sort of pot to put wet umbrellas in, whatever needs your particular climate indicates. Also valuable are table or chest to lay packages on as you enter, and a mirror hung over it to check your appearance as you leave the house. Some sort of appropriate lighting fixture or system is also needed, but the walls will play the starring role in this area of the home.

If the entrance hall is quite small and dark, the use of a foil paper will reflect light and make a contemporary hall seem larger. The use of mirror strips or squares will lighten and raise the ceiling and expand the walls of a dreary little hall at the entrance to the living room.

The entrance hall can be quite festive, and strike a bold note of color and pattern; large squares of black and white flooring tiles set on the diagonal add visual interest and a grand illusion of spaciousness to a narrow hall. A famous designer of fabrics designed and decorated a long narrow hall leading into in his apartment with a bold black-and-white patterned carpeting. One wall of the hall was painted black and the other side was painted white, and the effect was exciting and space-creating. Carefully designed Supergraphics (see Manufacturers List) in bright colors or with varying values and intensities of one color can lead the eye around corners and up and over low ceilings and break the boundaries of a dull little hallway.

The warmth of natural materials adds textural interest to this entryway. The dark paneled wooden door is real wood, but the brick wall is a masonry paneling that captures the natural appearance, texture, and color-veining of weathered brick. (Masonite Corporation).

Entrance halls are fine places for grouping pictures over benches or chests, or a whole wall of family photographs covering the area going up the stairs.

Perhaps the problem with your entrance hall is that it does not exist, and one walks directly into the living room. In this case, you must create some sort of welcoming area through illusion. A mirrored screen folding out from the wall to form a partition would work splendidly, or perhaps a chest or divider made up of modular cabinets or shelves with plants set on top under a grow-light fixture. A screen covered with an exciting fabric or paper, or a wall hanging, can also define the area. A partition of natural wood louvers, either in the traditional shutter form or the newer vertical ones, serves as a good warm accent. Usually, the builder has included at least a closet by the front door and through the use of color in paint or wallpaper or both, or woodpaneling, you can frame the closet area to create a welcoming space.

HALLWAYS

Corridors and hallways present some of the same problems as the entrance hall and are solved by some of the same wall treatments. The main problem with corridors and hallways is to make them interesting, appear wider, lighter, and to help them coordinate with the rest of the rooms of the house. In some cases the hallway is the coordinating element for all the home's diverse areas. In general, most hallways and corridors are too straight and narrow with no interesting nooks and crannies in which to place furniture or even windows or window seats. Small-scale narrow chests, consoles or wall tables, hanging shelves and mirrors, plant stands, slim benches, skinny chairs and so on are about as much furniture as you will be able to fit in fairly recently built hallways. Sometimes it is possible to have a wall of bookshelves and other storage in the hallway.

Hallways are great places for hanging pictures and assortments of family portraits, photographs, and other hangable memorabilia; placing it all on one wall is particularly good. Certain collections, such as clocks, old keys, antique maps, and other such items that need close scrutiny add a great deal of interest. (Collections have a way of multiplying and here is one way to obtain more space for displaying them. If they are not hangable as such, perhaps they can be mounted together in frames or wall-hung cases). Corridors make good art galleries also, but remember that you cannot step too far back to get the

An entrance hall of contemporary elegance. The long vertical redwood paneling soars from floor to ceiling, softened by carpeted stairtreads and a large plant. The white ceiling and tall windows add to the feeling of great space. This arrangement requires art work bold enough to hold its own, as seen through the hallway (California Redwood Association).

An entryway becomes an introduction to family interests and tastes when collections or shelves of treasured items are displayed.

full effect of a large poster or painting; these are more effective in a large entrance hall or living room.

There are various ways in which to make the hallways appear larger, lighter, and wider. Foil wallpaper on walls and ceilings, either plain or patterned, give the feeling of infinite space. Mirror squares used on the ceiling and along one wall will lighten and brighten the area. Painting one wall a light, bright, receding color (green) and the other wall and ceiling white, will create spaciousness. An interesting, wandering-line type of Supergraphic that wanders up and down and in and out over shiny white walls will direct the eye wherever it goes and detract from the narrow space. Track lighting which floods one wall with light will make the wall appear to disappear. Shiny white-backgrounded wallpaper, with a large airy pattern in one color, works well. Another simple and effective treatment for a long dark hallway is to paint the walls white and each door a different color, extending the door color up the wall over the door to the ceiling and, for more illusion, across the ceiling, creating interesting, succeeding bands of color down the hall. Each color could be linked to the color scheme of the room within. Illusion is the name of the game, and with a little imagination and your own personal creativity let loose, that dull little hallway is no more!

An effective dining or game area can be created off the living room by the use of a striking wall covering either on a wall or mounted on a screen that serves as a room divider (Jack Denst Designs, Inc.).

LIVING ROOMS

The next area of the home under discussion is the living room. The role of the living room appears to be in a state of change at the moment. We no longer have the separate formal front parlor reserved only for company, calls from the minister, and wakes, plus the separate and formal dining room and the less formal living or keeping room (or informal "back parlor") of our ancestors. The lack of space, lack of servants and therefore necessarily more informal style of living, have changed all this. The servants have been replaced by machines and all that space has disappeared along with the low cost of living (and building). There are still some people who are fortunate enought to have separate dining rooms and who use them frequently, but in general those who have them use them only for special occasions. The family dining is done in part of the family room or a large living room-kitchen. Generally the more formal dining and entertaining is done in a dining "L" off the living room or in a space created by illusion within the living room itself.

Dining Areas

Creating a dining area out of the living room where there is an L-shaped or other defined area off the living room can be done, with imagination, several different ways. The problem is to create a separate space and yet coordinate it to the living room. Part of this comes with a continuity of style or feeling in the furniture, and an area rug is useful, but the wall treatment has the most power. The dining area can be wallpapered, wood paneled, or painted an accent color to set it apart from the living area. If there is no defined space set aside for dining you must create one much in the same manner discussed for creating an entrance hall out of the living room. The furniture from the living area can help here, such as the use of a grouping of sofa and loveseat, with the sofa

This living room arrangement maximizes the potential conversation and comfort possibilities around the fireplace. The shag area rug contrasts with and shows off the hardwood floors and wood paneling (U.S. Plywood).

The open area in this large living room has been sectioned off for different activities: in foreground, bar-shelf dining setup; in the far corner, a game table that can also be used for eating; in the center, framed by paneling, a sofa-chair group (U.S. Plywood).

against the wall with a corner table and the loveseat placed next to the corner table at a right angle to the sofa wall, thus dividing the room. A mirrored wall can help to define and visually enlarge your dining area. Most houses have now placed the family dining area in the family room and kitchen, with or without a separate formal dining room used only on "State" occasions. We will discuss these two other options later, and now return to the living room.

Activities

For most people the living room is for entertaining, for conversation and evening parties. So major requirements are an aura of warmth, comfort, and hospitality, with seating pieces and tables placed in groupings congenial to conversation. Hopefully some of the owner's personality will be evident and this will not contain merely an attractive but sterile seating area. Living rooms are good places for quiet activities such as reading, writing letters, listening to classical music and so on. A fireplace always creates a gracious, cozy atmosphere, and offers a dynamic center of attraction for the living room.

Material selection for certain effects

Unless you have a very formal period-type living room with a Georgian painted paneled wainscoting with formal patterned wallpaper above, as is traditional, patterned wallpaper is not the best wall treatment for the living room. The size of the area and its usage call more for color and texture. A texture wallpaper, such as grasscloth or burlap simulation would be more effective. There is an exception to this and that is the wallpaper mural on one wall, which can be very suitable depending upon the subject matter and the furnishings. It can not only be a focal point, but can really push that wall back to give the illusion of more space.

Wood paneling, brick and natural stone are all good wall coverings for the living room. The warmth of natural materials adds to the feeling of conviviality. Wood paneling installed vertically gives a feeling of height to the room, while the newer method of horizontal installation adds width to the wall, and often a feeling of restful calm. The natural tones of wood are better used on one wall (fireplace wall, perhaps) of such a large area, or at least should be relieved by some white areas, as an all wood-paneled room can be too dark. Natural wood ceilings with white walls are most attractive, if your ceiling is high enough. A pickled, bleached or painted wood paneling can be used effectively for the entire wall treatment,

This apartment living room utilizes shade cloth and wall covering in an interesting window-wall treatment. The shade cloth forms a series of sliding panels, which are flanked by a pair of stationary panels featuring a large-scaled pattern of bright flowers. These were created by applying fabric by iron-on method to a specially developed shade cloth. The entire effect is of a continuous, unified series of vertical rectangles that frame the window view (Window Shade Mfrs. Assn.).

The furniture grouping here centers on the dramatic fireplace, which is starkly set off by vertical paneling (Georgia-Pacific).

An interesting effect has been achieved in this living room with an abstract marbelized wall covering design. The suedelike sofa upholstery, the wood tables, and the plants, pottery and carving accessories, all add to the natural, back-to-the-earth aura. Note the unusual shelf with art objects and plants; it carries your eye around the corner and unifies the seating group (Katzenback and Warren, Inc.).

past the windows to cover the entire wall, all these, providing you have picked a light, receding color or very pale value of a warm color, will make the room appear larger.

Another way to make the living room seem larger is, again, through the use of mirrors or foil paper. Mirror squares or panels or foil paper can be used on the window wall very effectively. If you have a group of two or three windows separated by strips of wall space, these spaces covered with mirrors or folding screens of mirror from floor to ceiling on either side of a large sliding window door, will add to the apparent size and brightness of the room. It gives the illusion of one continuous, luminous window wall. Many condominium apartment living rooms open out onto balconies and a mirror or mirror squares cover the wall at right angles to the window wall and extend if possible out onto a wall of the balcony. One thing to remember is that mirrors reflect, naturally, what is in front of them and you must be careful about a lot of leggy furniture, such as a dining table and chairs, being reflected unattractively; a foil that reflects only vaguely, yet has a reflective quality, would be more effective in this case. An unattractive structural portion of wall jutting out can be visually eliminated by placing a mirror on the projecting surface. The use of mirrors and foil papers can be an extremely powerful tool for illusion, but you must be sure of what illusion you are trying to create and perhaps experiment a little before you make any permanent installation. There is a tendency for the use of mirrors and foil papers to be too cold and brittle for everyday living…it is possible to overdo a good thing.

Wall accessories

The living room offers an ideal display area for paintings, prints, and collections. One large painting or graphic with a lot of punch can set the tone for the whole room, or a well arranged grouping of pictures, sometimes combined with clocks or other hangable art objects, can be a marvelous focal point for a conversational seating group. There are a few practical rules to help you in hanging pictures. In general, pictures should be hung near a furniture grouping or over a chest or table. If hung alone on a wall either the one picture or the whole group of paintings should be large enough to visually fill that particular wall space. It is permissible to hang prints in steps going up the wall, if you are going up the stair wall, or if you are trying to call attention to something, or if you are fitting around a chair and table with lamp grouping; but, please do not hang the paintings in steps leading up into a corner or away from your center of interest. It will create a feeling of unbalance and restlessness.

The Green Room, a Federal Parlor in the White House, was renovated in 1961 to look as it might have during the time of Presidents John Adams and Thomas Jefferson. Late in 1962 the walls were recovered with a moss-green watered silk, thus providing a more appropriate background and setting for the ornate, period framing of the art (courtesy of the White House Historical Association; photograph taken by the National Geographic Society).

however. A brick or fieldstone fireplace that extends itself into the whole wall is another successful wall treatment, as is textured paint.

An attractive living room seating arrangement is that of a conversation pit entirely lined with the same carpeting as used on the floor. A comfortable cushioned seating can be custom-built into the conversation pit and, with a large square coffee table in the middle it will be cozy. The carpeting used in the conversation pit can be extended up 1 or 2 walls for warmth, comfort, and sound absorption.

Some of today's living rooms are not as large an area as they might be, and could use a little illusion. Painting the woodwork the same shade as the walls, selecting a carpet the same color but a slightly darker value than the walls, selecting a plain drapery fabric that matches the walls (but has textural interest) and extending the drapery

Stripes and floral wall covering in coordinated colors combine for a cheerful little dining room. The chair rail and baseboard painted in white help set off the two patterns (Colombus Coated Fabrics).

The Southwest atmosphere has been created with earth-toned colors and natural textures of Mexican tiles, Navajo blankets, wood beam accents, and painted and natural adobe walls (Majestic Fireplaces).

If you will be viewing your artwork sitting down, then it should be hung lower and closer to the top of the sofa or whatever is in your grouping. If you will be viewing it from a standing position, then it can be hung a little higher. You must look at each wall as a composition, just as a painter does, formed by your furnishings, architectural features, and any wall decoration you care to add. There must be balance to the whole composition and your eye must be directed in the way you consciously intend it to be, just as in a painting. The single large painting or the group of smaller prints will give a certain feeling of mass and weight, and must be hung to balance the entire wall.

One way to ease the pain and strain of putting together an interesting group of artwork or of decorative wall-hung accessories is to first make a little sketch of the wall you are working on, pretty much to scale (maybe on graph paper) and draw in the furniture, windows, and so on...then add the pictures, etc. you are planning on. If you can assemble the group of paintings or prints into some sort of geometric shape such as a square, rectangle, triangle or circle for some sort of cohesion, it will help. Then you must analyze the visual weight of the arrangement, taking into account large and small pieces, and that darker paintings are heavier than those with bright or pastel colors. Even the frames enter into the composition and must be considered part of the scheme. If you are assembling such a grouping over a table with a lamp or over a sofa with lamps on tables near by, leave a space for the lamps, do not hang anything behind these objects. Superimposing the lamp over your grouping will destroy the composition. The lamp or whatever is in front must be included in the design.

Collections are good wall accessories in the living room. Collections of pewter mugs, African carvings, blue Bristol ware in an interesting wall-hung cupboard, artists sketches, minerals arranged on open shelves and so on, all give your living space that special sparkle which reflects your own personality.

In selecting accessories and accents for your walls, there are many points to consider and choices to be made. First and foremost, relate it to where it will go. Quite often this is no problem because the object or painting came first, with the room decorated around it to accent your treasure. You must also consider color and whether it will fit with your color scheme, or again perhaps the color scheme stems from the graphic or painting. Is the size in scale with the other furnishings in your living room (or any room, for that matter) and is the style or period in harmony with your other furnishings? Everything doesn't have to be of the same period, unless you really want it to be; things from different styles and periods mix very nicely if color, proportion, texture,

Wall plaques, wicker hangings and lots of greenery combine with the natural beauty of authentically woodgrained paneling to give this contemporary informal dining area off the kitchen a great deal of charm (Masonite Corporation).

pattern either blend well or contrast in an interesting but not shocking manner. Eighteenth century New England has shown us the compatibility of Oriental rugs, china, furniture and accessories with the colonial furnishings of that time. The Southwest has assimilated the beauty of Navaho rugs and native adobe in with the Spanish heritage shown in beautifully carved dark wooden chests, combined with the mellow handmade Mexican floor tiles and all put together in a comfortable, casual setting.

DINING ROOMS

If you are fortunate enough to have a separate dining room and plan to use it, then you are in for an enjoyable and creative decorating job. A meal is a festive occasion, and everything, including the interior design of the dining room itself, should contribute to this pleasure. Here is another room in the house where you can really let yourself go and create any illusion you wish. Wallpaper can really come into its own here—murals, scenics, flocked damask (also good for its acoustical qualities), or stylized florals traditionally placed over a chair rail and painted dado or used in panels formed with wood mold-

ing. White-painted, wood-paneled walls suit a cheerful French Provincial dining room with a collection of favorite plates hung in a wall grouping over the buffet. Try mirrors, mirrored walls and mirrored self-stick squares, foil wallpapers, murals, exciting and dramatic color schemes, matching wallpaper and fabric for the draperies, a print fabric or luxurious velvet or suede cloth applied to the walls...or green painted walls with white wood strips applied to the wall like a garden lattice wall to give an outdoor feeling, especially with the addition of a plant stand filled with greenery (if you don't wish to go this far there are many wallpapers with a white lattice pattern on various colored backgrounds, some with the addition of green leaves, that can create the same illusion for you).

If you use mirrors to add dimension, an especially attractive chandelier should be chosen since it will be reflected in the wall-mirror.

Almost anything goes in the dining room if it creates the illusion that you wish as your background for entertaining or just congenial family meals, aside from some color or theme to connect it with the rest of your living space and your family's personality.

95

The horizontal stripes seem to flow around the recessed bathtub, to unify and visually enlarge this bathroom (American Standard photo).

*For more specifics on bathroom arrangements, consult *Book of Successful Bathrooms* by Joseph F. Schram.

BATHROOMS

It used to be that the guest or downstairs bathroom was the only really fancy one in the house. It wasn't used too often and could have all those nice non-scrubbable papers or other impractical things in it. Now, of course, you have the new vinyl-coated or vinyl wall coverings, not to mention the beautiful ceramic tiles that are a far cry from the orchid with black trim and peach with brown trim of a generation ago. Even wood paneling can be plastic-coated for use on bathroom walls, or simulated in plastic laminate. In other words, now all the bathrooms in the house can be up to company standards, and then some. Here again, in available wall coverings, we find practical, colorful, luxurious choices. Mirror-doored medicine cabinets, or a whole wall of mirrors over the sink counter with the cabinet on a side wall, or a mirrored ceiling, all enlarge the apparent size and reflective light in the bathroom. Many more architectural materials, such as wood, brick, fieldstone, marble are being used, often with the plants. Sometimes if the climate is right, you can have a private little sunning patio off the bathroom, available through a sliding glass door, or just a little garden visible to the bathroom but screened by a fence or brick wall outside.*

The new foil papers and textured vinyl wall coverings have added such excitement to the possibilities of illusion. The new ceramic tiles run from very natural, handmade-looking ceramic pieces to two-dimensional sculptured tiles with which you can arrange your own design, to brightly glazed tiles—some with striking designs that can be arranged into many different larger designs. Because most bathrooms are fairly small, it is best to use the same wall covering throughout. This is not a positive rule, however. In choosing bathroom wall covering it is a good idea to select a material, color, or pattern compatible with the decorating scheme used in adjoining rooms. This can be accomplished with color, textures, and choice of materials. Wall surfaces commonly found in bathrooms include decorative plastic laminates, ceramic tile, plastic tile, enamel-painted plaster or gypsum wallboard, and vinyl wall coverings. Wallpaper and fabric can be purchased with a washable and waterproof surface, or waterproof treatment can be applied following installation. Generally, wallpaper is more practical in lavatories and powder rooms where moisture is not produced by tub or shower bathing.

Most bathroom walls are finished in pastel or light colors. If you wish to use a dark color or a simulated dark wood finish, keep in mind that this will absorb more natural and artificial light. You may need additional lighting to compensate for the dark walls.

This compartmented bathroom relies on a clean and crisp combination of different patterns printed on vinyl wall covering. The use of the different patterns works because they are all geometrics, and all the same color (American Standard photo).

The Old World atmosphere in this compartmented bathroom results from the rough-hewn wood beams, used to accent a fresh, large floral print, in combination with the parquet floor (Universal-Rundle photo).

A restful but imaginative bedroom. The interesting alcove has been created for the bed by using a companion floral to the plaid, in what used to be a closet. The colors are bright pastels suitable to any sex or age group, in a fabric-backed, plastic-coated wall covering (Columbus Coated Fabrics).

Matching wallpaper and fabric in a design of Ivy Geranium are used on the walls, in draperies and bedspread. The same pattern used all over makes the room appear larger and also hides architectural imperfections. The lightweight white-painted rattan furniture enhances the feminine, personalized effect (Katzenbach and Warren, Inc.).

BEDROOMS

Guest rooms

And now we'll go on to the bedrooms, starting with the guest bedroom, which usually has a dual or even triple purpose. The guestroom-study-den is the most popular perhaps, or the guest-sewing or hobby room. What this means is that the ambiance must be one of hospitality and broad appeal. As a dual-purpose room the bedding involved will either fold away into the wall, or will be the equivalent of a box-spring and mattress with a tailored removable cover, or the mattress itself upholstered in attractive fabric to serve as a sofa and the bedding made up on top of it when it is time to convert into a bedroom. A guestroom-study-den room is not usually very large. One way to counteract this is to use a colorful matching wallpaper and fabric in a small geometric print, using the fabric for the windows and upholstery, plus a monochromatic color scheme. This creates a hospitable atmosphere and makes the room appear larger. The guestroom or study-den is, naturally, the perfect place for bookshelves filled with books, art objects and other collectibles. These cabinets and shelves can be spotlighted with a lighting track installed on the ceiling. The back wall of the shelves can be lined with mirrors to add a feeling of spaciousness and to enable you to see the back of art objects. Cork and carpet tiles with adhesive backing are, applied to the wall, cozy and good sound absorbers for peace and quiet.

Family bedrooms

And now we come to the family bedrooms, which can be treated in a more individual fashion. It would be advisable to link the rooms through the use of one color or another in that agreed-upon family color scheme mentioned earlier. Aside from that, this is where the different personalities living under one roof can really express themselves!

Let us first consider the master bedroom, usually a shared bedroom and therefore it should be neither too frilly and feminine, nor too rough and masculine. The Master Bedroom should be a restful, comfortable room, a real haven and place to get away from it all. Warm and appealing textures, a calm and relaxed color scheme (see color lists in previous chapter), comfortable and attractive bedding, hopefully room for a small seating area...a real plus would be a fireplace in the bedroom. Bookshelves are nice also.

Since most people prefer a patterned wallpaper in the bedroom, this seems to be the place to discuss what

A thousand clowns cheer up this young child's bedroom. The furniture is a simple design that can be used when the child grows older, at which point the wallpaper can be replaced by a plain-colored texture that will leave the striped window area as an accent (Columbus Coated Fabrics).

This red and white Bandana print wallpaper adds a touch of gaiety to a young girl's bedroom. A little bed "closet" reminiscent of Britanny is created by the striking white beams and white-with-red curtains. White-painted wood floors add to the country feeling (Thibaut Wallcoverings).

Posters have become popular recently as wall art, and are ideal in the young man's bedroom or informal apartment. The vertical installation of the paneling, extended up and over a lighting soffit, gives an impression of unbroken height (U.S. Plywood).

kind of pictures or paintings or prints to hang on a patterned wall. Pattern on pattern is a challenge, but with a few hints it becomes an exciting challange. The main thing to remember is that you must have some common color in the patterns that you are combining, and that one pattern must be larger than the other; a small print hung against a small patterned wallpaper is generally a waste of effort. It is not necessary to match periods, in fact it is more fun not to most of the time, however there must be some sort of compatibility of feeling among the patterns combined. A modern abstract print against a flower-sprigged wallpaper looks awful, but if the floral is stylized, almost geometric, and if the colors go well together, the modern abstract might just work against that background. There is again the matter of scale and balance to consider. As for the frames, they must of course enhance the picture, not match the furniture.

The adjoining master bath dressing rooms should all coordinate with the bedroom, and be used if possible to frame the bedroom design.

99

A corner arrangement of the bed allows more room and individuality in a small room. A stylized floral print sets off the large lithographs. White molding at the ceiling and around the wallpaper door become part of the room's overall, continuous pattern (Magnavox photo).

For the small child's bedroom, the room must be bright and colorful and yet have dignity. A baby should have something bright to look at from his crib, either on the wall or ceiling—a painted mural, or wallpaper cut-outs, or wallpaper on the ceiling. Children should be able to draw on a designated part of their wall space. There is blackboard wallboard, or green blackboard paint that you can paint on the wall.

Put in shelves for toys and books, and perhaps a winding, wiggling Supergraphic painted on the wall—or a rainbow painted on the wall to double as headboard. Most of the furniture, such as desk and chests, could be built in, leaving more room for play. Simplicity, bright colors, easy maintenance, and a touch of whimsy are the main things to keep in mind when decorating the child's bedroom.

As the children get older and into their teens, their rooms need to be more individualized. In fact, you will be

lucky to get in there to decorate the bedroom. It would be best to have the older child make selections and maybe choose some of the painting or other decorating, with a little help and guidance from parents. The teen-age and older children of the family need sound conditioning …as much as you can contrive with carpet squares, cork paneling which doubles as tack-up board, burlap wall covering, and so on to take care of the radio and/or Hi Fi or both, and maybe even a TV set! From then on it really should be their choice, within the budget. Posters are great wall decorations and so are record album covers. Wood paneling is popular.

Maybe your daughter desires a four-poster bed and all the traditional flower-sprigged ruffles. If you don't have room for that big bed you can create the same feeling with a wooden four-posted frame covered with wallpaper or painted to match the wallpaper.

This family room was converted from a double garage. The bay window replaced the garage doors and the walls were finished with V-joint Western Wood board paneling. The paneling, brick hearth and mantle, country furniture, and Franklin stove, all contribute to the room's theme decor (Western Wood Products Association).

KITCHEN AND FAMILY AREAS

The kitchen and family rooms in today's homes seem to all flow together with an informal eating area in one big living space. A lot of women prefer to entertain this way, so that they can talk to their family and/or guests while they are preparing meals.

The family room (and to some extent all this will apply to recreation rooms also) should be a cheerful, comfortable living space. Easy maintenance is essential because this is the room in which the family seems to spend most of their time. A fireplace is ideal for a family room, either built into the wall, or a Franklin Stove, or a modern metal free-standing fireplace. A wood-burning one is preferable but the electric log and gas ones are effective also. In general no more than two different materials should be used in constructing the fireplace, such as brick with a copper hood, or fieldstone with a heavy wooden beam for the mantle. And speaking of beams, the

Tudor Beam and Stucco look is quite popular in family rooms, or just the heavy exposed beams in the ceiling reminiscent of pioneer days.

Wood paneling is good in family rooms, but should be tempered with white walls or bright colors here and there to keep the interior from being very dark. Brick walls, textured wall coverings, carpet tiles, cork panels, family bulletin boards, family photographs and artwork, all have a place in the family room. Posters & Supergraphics are also possibilities.

The dining area of the family room is usually near a window under an attractive hanging light fixture. I don't believe it is necessary to divide this area off either visually or physically, as it might be in a living room. It is important to make the whole area hang together in feeling and in color.

The kitchen should be efficient and light. Whether you have oak or fruitwood-carved wood or wood-laminate cabinets, an old fashioned kitchen look or sleek, gleaming stainless steel and formica, you can find a wall

A basement-recreation room with something for everyone. The soft-neutral gray paneling harmonizes with almost any color scheme, and is light enough to brighten an underground area. The paneling features the graining and characteristic "pecky" marks of one of the world's rarest and most costly woods (Masonite Corporation).

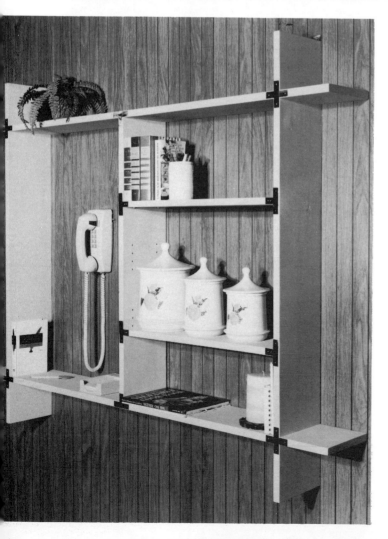

covering to suit your mood. The oldfashioned kitchen can have a sculptured plastic wall covering simulating real brick, and the modern kitchen can have a geometric design printed on foil vinyl wall covering, or a simulated burlap textured vinyl.

Another idea is to use one of the new self-stick vinyl floor tile squares on the floor and also on the wall between the countertop and the wall-hung cabinets. Ceramic tile is one of your best choices in the kitchen. It can be used on the floor, the countertop, and the walls most attractively and durably.

There are many possibilities in patterned wallpapers for kitchens. Now that the kitchen has opened up to be part of a larger whole used by many people, it is probably best to avoid the very cute kitcheny designs that used to be popular when the kitchen was a separate entity. It needs more dignity now. The patterns can still be gay and contain flowers or vegetables and so on, but in a more a sophisticated fashion and often with the use of a coordinated stripe or plaid in the family room (and the utility-laundry-mud room if it is adjoining).

A kitchen organizer adds design and three-dimensionality to the wall. This unit serves as a telephone center, cooking library, storage shelf, and still has room for plants and knick-knacks. It is mounted on Marlite prefinished hardboard planks.

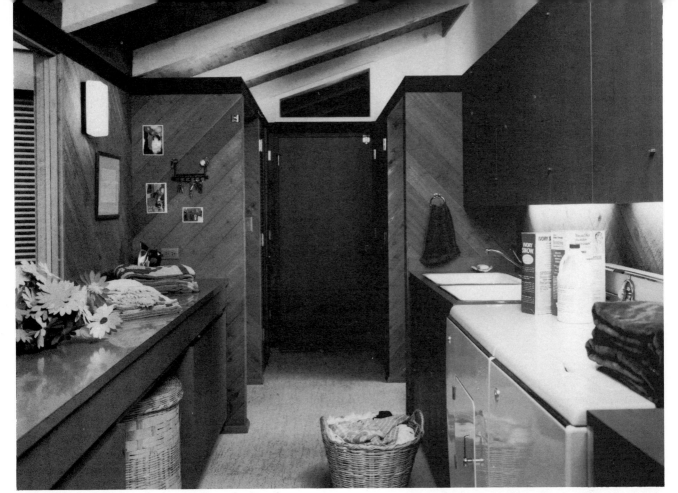

Lucky is the homemaker who has a gallery-plan laundry center such as this one! Notice the western cedar board paneling, applied diagonally for interest. The exposed beams and the walls painted white above the paneling emphasize the room's size (Western Wood Products Association).

EFFICIENCY APARTMENTS

The one-room efficiency apartments should be at least mentioned in this book. The problems here are how to divide up the different living spaces and how to make these areas appear larger and more spacious, how to coordinate the color scheme and make it all hang together. First you must analyze your particular problem and decide upon the atmosphere you wish to achieve and then use the best possible method from the many we have discussed.

Perhaps Aleksandra Kasuba mentioned in the chapter on color, texture, and pattern, has the right idea after all with her knitted-nylon stretch fabric areas, with only the simplest of furnishings and the lovely shaggy rugs and pillows and glowing light...beauty, texture, comfort, versatility, division of space that can be changed as needed. At least it is something to think about and to spur you to reflect on your own lifestyle, and how you express it in your wall decorations.

This whimsical geometric design of this wall covering proves to be, upon close inspection, "Mason Jars," as it is named. The wall covering has also been used to cover the window shades. The addition of strategically placed wood beams and a hanging plant effectively divide off a dining area from the kitchen (Style-Tex vinyl wall covering; photo courtesy of Wallcovering Industry Bureau).

3. Hanging Wall Covering Like a Pro

Introduction

Wall covering materials offer both beauty and variety to the home decorator, with less disarray and expense than many other home improvements.

But unfortunately, to take advantage of most of these decorative opportunities a decorator, either professional or do-it-yourselfer, must sometimes select patterns available only on delicate or heavy materials. Very often, homeowners are reluctant to select these highly desirable and attractive but risky first choices. They know that they run a high probability of failure, and that professional installation of costly materials is also expensive.

So they have to settle for less expensive although often still lovely second choices, made of sturdier materials. These they can either install themselves, or have installed inexpensively by an ordinary journeyman painter who also doubles as a wallpaper-hanger whenever he has the chance.

While this section will aim to improve techniques used in ordinary paperhanging, primary attention will be directed toward expanding the skills of the handyperson-around-the-house, so that he or she will be prepared to cope with the more desirable materials which, without this information, would be beyond their capabilities. Specific suggestions will be given for particular materials. The methods and techniques used by leading professionals will be described. Photos and diagrams will be used to demonstrate difficult procedures, since experience gathered at lecture demonstrations for professional paperhangers has shown that seeing it is more effective than just hearing or reading about it.

The first three chapters of this section cover tools, surface preparation, matching and trimming and, in general, getting ready for final application. Read these chapters carefully and in their entirety. They will cover procedures common to most materials as well as some steps required by only a few. The short time needed to master these steps will make the rest of the learning experience easy—even fun.

The final chapter deals with application of nine major classes of wall-covering materials. Each class has been divided into types. The reader need only read the sections pertaining to the class of material he or she will be using.

In a few instances, the reader may be advised to hire a professional—or to use another product—because high costs of some materials, such as certain silks or orientals, coupled with their delicacy and high probability of failure, heighten the risk factor.

The techniques presented here are the same techniques taught budding professionals; a reasonable amount of attention will make it possible for you to achieve the same results.

The consumer applying his own wall covering—or interested in having his professionally applied job done right, should remember at all times that a wall covering is a temporary wall facing—not meant for the ages. It has to go up; it also has to come down—easily, preferably.

Remember that not only is the wall covering you select all-important, but so is the adhesive and the condition of the wall. The right adhesive on the properly prepared wall will, later on, mean the difference between a simple removal and a traumatic hassle.

Tools

For both the serious do-it-yourselfer who expects to do a lot of wall covering, and the professional who will need all the efficiency aids available, more tools will be needed than for a handyperson who needs one or two rooms redecorated. Both workers are covered in the accompanying lists of wall-covering tools.

Minimum	Maximum
Two horses and plywood for trimming and pasting	Box table—6′x3′
Cutting board—1 inch board 1 ft. x4 ft.	Zinc plate
Yard stick—for measuring and as cutting guide	Straight edge, or 6 ft. ruler
Level—4 foot or plumb bob	Plumb bob
Scissors—any kind	8″ shears
Brushes—	Brushes—same as minimum
One 12″ smoothing brush, soft pure bristle	
One 12″ smoothing brush, short stiff bristle (or nylon)	
One 12″ smoothing brush, soft pure bristle	
One 3″ paint brush for pasting top of wall	
Rollers—	Rollers—
¾ inch plastic for rolling	One ¼″ steel for rolling
One 7 to 7⅜″ nap paint roller for pasting	One ¾″ steel for rolling
One 9 to 9⅜″ nap paint roller for pasting	One 2″ steel for rolling
	(Pasting rollers same as minimum)
Sponge	Several sponges

Minimum	Maximum
Bucket	Two buckets
Several single-edge razor blades and razor knife	Same as minimum, plus special wall-protecting cutter for heavy materials
Hair dryers—1,000 watts (if job involves new strippable polyester backing)	Same as minimum
Drop cloths, or brown paper	Drop cloths
Sandpaper, medium	Sandpaper and sandpaper block
Screwdriver for removing switch plates, etc.	Same as minimum
Patching plaster, or spackling compound	Same as minimum
Stepladder, preferably two with plank for scaffold	Same as minimum
Water tray for prepasted wall covering	Same as minimum

The proper tools are necessary in order to achieve a professional-looking job.

Success Needs
a Sound Surface

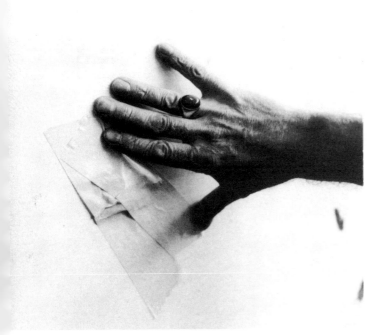

Masking tape should be applied to painted wall and pulled up to see if adhesive and wall covering is likely to cause paint to lift underneath the wall covering, and ruin the job.

Loose walls, like loose living, lead to trouble. So Rule 1 in hanging wall coverings:

Scrape anything that's loose, or potentially loose, off the wall.

That rule covers loose paint, loose wall covering, dust, grease, sand-filled paints, and anything else that could cause the new covering to peel off.

Obviously, if the adhesive will not stick to the surface, the wall covering will soon loosen. So Rule 2 is:

Make certain that the adhesive will stick to the wall, or whatever is on the wall.

Here's what we mean. Glossy paints are usually very hard because they contain more resin (which is hard) than they do pigment (which is soft), so adhesives often can't penetrate and bond. Medium-grit sandpaper can be used to roughen the hard surface (do not use coarse grit sandpaper). You can now, however, buy an emulsion bonding agent that does as well as sanding. It dries in 20 to 60 minutes and you can hang wall coverings right after the solution dries. It even works over ceramic tile, formica, and hard epoxy paint. It goes on white, but dries clear.

Even flat paints may prove to be troublesome if they are the cheap types often used by apartment owners. They may contain too much cheap filler-pigments, and your adhesive may cause this paint to lift under the wall covering. If you are suspicious, test flat paints by taping a wet ball of cotton to the wall for ten minutes, and then observing whether or not the paint softens. If it does, prime it with an enamel undercoater, or the emulsion bonding agent described above. Make certain that the surface beneath the covering has a dull finish.

Any time your surface appears to be absorbent, use an oil-based or latex primer-sealer to keep the adhesive from being sucked into the surface and failing to hold. Shellac is acceptable, but is not as well regarded as primer-sealers. If the surface is extremely rough, you may have to use a lining paper, which we'll talk about later.

In general, old wallpaper should be removed, but there are exceptions if you know how to recognize them. Here is Rule 3:

Remove old wallpaper unless it adheres firmly to the surface, especially where the seams join and where the edges join the ceiling, or at any protruding surface such as a window sill or molding.

You can tell whether or not the covering adheres firmly by cutting out two square feet of the wall covering you plan to use. Apply paste to half of it. Apply the entire square, which means that one half will flap loose since it has no paste. Let the square stand overnight. Next morning, or when you get an opportunity, tear off the unpasted section, which will pull up the pasted section as well. If the old wall covering beneath the newly pasted part comes off with it, then you know the old wall covering has to be removed.

Another detail to watch out for is the presence of a plastic coating on old wallpaper. If this is the case, simply use an alkyd primer-sealer before applying the new wall covering. Use a similar coating over old wallpapers that have become dry and chalky.

In removing old wallpapers, try saturating the old covering with water. If you are lucky and the material can be readily saturated with water, then you can easily scrape it off. Commercial wallpaper removers heighten better water penetration and speed the job. Also most cities have stores that rent wallpaper steamers for large-scale removal. *Caution:* Never use a steamer near fine cabinets, fine furniture, or fine floors. Experienced contractors use them only in empty rooms, with open windows.

If you are trying to remove a foil covering or one overcoated with a water-resistant material, use sandpaper or an abrasive of some kind to bite shallowly into the surface to reach the water-absorbent material. Then saturate, using a light mist from a hand sprayer, or a sponge, or whatever is handy.

Don't forget that removing the paper is just the first part of the job. The adhesive on the wall must also be worked off, usually with hot water applied with a gentle abrasive pad. And you definitely want to be careful about gouging the walls.

Spackling compound or similar filler should be used at this point to smooth out any gouges or depressions, which may be apparent under certain wall coverings, particularly under shiny materials.

For reasons of economy most walls today are made of plasterboard sections which, like plywood and all preformed wall components, are imperfectly joined. Small gaps of a fraction of an inch occur where these components meet. These gaps must be covered, usually with a tape topped by spackle. We now come to Rule 4:

Always tape and spackle joints between preformed wall components, and once the spackle is dry use a primer-sealer so the porous components won't suck in the adhesive, which would make it extremely difficult to remove the wall covering when its time has come.

Cover nailholes and other irregularities with spackle. Use paper tape over plasterboard; use fiberglass mesh over plywood.

If you will be applying wall covering over a newly plastered wall (which is extremely unlikely) don't apply any wall covering until you have determined, with a moisture meter, that the wall is dry. Since plaster is frequently highly alkaline, play safe and wash the wall with a solution of zinc sulfate—one pound to a gallon of water. Rinse with clear water and allow to dry thoroughly. Now comes Rule 5:

Size the wall before applying wall covering.

When the walls are sufficiently old or appear porous, or have old wallpaper with a fine dust or a powdered paint you can't completely remove, treat the area with a glue size or an emulsion bonding agent. (They are the same for this purpose; however, emulsion bonding agents can also be used over glossy surfaces for application of wall coverings.) Several types of size are offered. The first is a cold-water natural powder; the second is a jelled size; and the third is a synthetic powder, also activated by water. Also, any paste thinned with water, except wheat paste, can be used as a size.

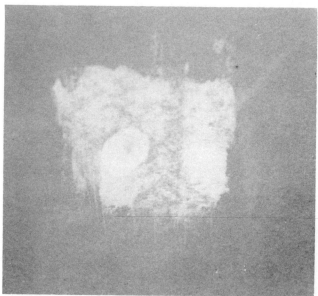

Nailheads in dry wall must be driven below the surface and smoothed over with spackling compound.

White lining paper corrects minor irregularities in surface and controls adhesive used for sensitive materials such as silk, grass cloth, and textiles. Acid-free lining paper (the roll beneath) is more expensive and whiter, but avoids possible harm. Leave ⅛ inch gap at ceiling, baseboard, window, and door casings.

Cold water natural powder and the jelled size entail a mildew risk under materials that do not breathe, such as vinyls, foil, and Mylar. The synthetic powder is protected against mildew.

Using a size is much less expensive than using a thinned paste. Professionals today sometimes use an emulsion bonding agent as a size, which allows easier removal of the wall coverings. The new improved synthetic adhesives now available are suitable for use as sizes as they are. If walls are too porous for hanging vinyls and other heavy materials, such as burlap, then the synthetic adhesive to be used for hanging should be thinned considerably and applied as a size.

Size assures a uniform perch for adhesive, eliminating inconsistent surfaces where some of the adhesive has penetrated the wall to a greater extent than in other areas.

And—Rule 6:

Whenever hand-print papers or other fine wall coverings require a heavy paste for proper hanging, or if costly papers are being used and the highest quality professional job is desired, then before hanging the wall covering a lining paper made of off-white paper stock should be pasted to the wall. This provides a partially absorbent and uniform surface, which will successfully receive most types of paste.

Lining paper also conceals surface irregularities which cannot otherwise be hidden. Its main purposes, however, are to absorb excess moisture from paste, acting like a blotter; to prevent popping of paint at the seams when paper is laid over old surfaces bearing numerous coats of paint; and to avoid lumpiness where heavy coats of adhesive are used.

Lining paper is sized with starch. Under a nonbreathing material such as vinyl or foil (as mentioned earlier) it may mildew. Using premixed vinyl adhesive reduces but does not eliminate the possibility of mildew.

Most commonly used lining papers come in widths of 20 to 27 inches. Adhesive must be applied to it, not the wall. A 38-inch nonacid lining paper, snow white, is used under silk and delicate papers. Wheat paste is recommended. This lining has no wet strength and must be applied very carefully.

A strippable lining paper, needing premixed adhesive, can be bought. However, getting the wall covering to stick to it is a problem. For easier future stripping, a lining canvas can be obtained. This light, sized cotton has been used mostly over plaster walls but may be used over other types as well.

Lining paper is easy to hang if a few pointers are observed. Strips should be precut as accurately as possible to avoid trimming at the wall. Be sure to leave about one-eighth of an inch of space between the edge of the lining paper and the ceiling.

This means cutting the strips one-eighth inch short.

Also trim this same amount short where the wall covering will adjoin door casings, window molding, and other nonwall surfaces. The same shorter cuts should be made at inner walls, to prevent blisters.

The reason for trimming short: the extra space allows the edges of the wall covering itself to bond to the wall, rather than to the lining paper. If the wall covering were to bond to the paper, the lining paper and covering might shrink at different rates, and lift.

For a lining paper adhesive, you should always use a premixed vinyl adhesive. If you have a glossy wall, use an emulsion bonding agent before applying adhesive.

NEVER OVERLAP THE EDGES OF LINING PAPER. Make a close joining but not necessarily a tight one. Use the same care you would when hanging paper.

These are all the rules we need for the actual surface itself and application of materials, but another, final rule is needed for handling electric switch plates. Here's Rule 7:

Remove electric switch plates, plug covers, and lighting fixtures before applying wall covering so that these may fit over the surface without showing any signs of a break in the surface.

This rule is self-evident. Cutting out areas in a strip of wall covering to allow for the emergence of switch plates or fixtures is obviously necessary. Care in measuring where the cut-outs are to be is essential, and cut-outs should be a little smaller than the actual fixture. Later, you may cover the fixtures using wall-covering pieces carefully matched to the pattern areas cut out earlier.

To summarize the preparation rules for wall covering:

1. Scrape off anything loose or likely to loosen later.
2. Make certain that adhesive will stick to the wall or whatever is on it.
3. Remove old wallpaper unless it adheres firmly to the surface, particularly at the edges.
4. Always tape and spackle joints between preformed wall components such as plasterboard, plywood, and fiberglass.
5. Porous old walls, or dusty paint, or old wall covering should be sized prior to covering.
6. Whenever fine wall covering requires heavy paste, be certain to apply lining paper to the wall prior to application.
7. Remove electric switch plates, plug covers and fixtures prior to hanging wallcovering.

Matching, Cutting, and Pasting

Now that we have gone over how to prepare walls correctly, a few easy steps remain. These require a minimum of attention before we begin application of material.

First, we have to decide whether we have a straight-across pattern—which simply means that the design, whatever it is, runs right straight across from one strip of applied paper to the next. For example, if we lay paper from one roll next to paper from another roll with the same pattern, we would have the same elements of the design repeated in any straight line drawn, or imagined, across the wall. That's why it's called a straight pattern.

You will notice that every roll of wall covering has what are known as *match points*. If you didn't have them for guides you would be in a bad way because you would have a helter skelter arrangement on the wall. In a straight-across pattern, you line up the match points and find that everything to the right of the match point is the same as everything to the left.

In what we call a *drop-match pattern,* once you line up the join marks, you will find that the first strip has the

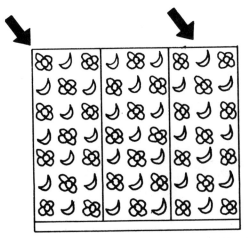

These three strips illustrate a drop-match pattern. Note that every other strip is the same at the top. (Drawing courtesy of National Decorating Products Association).

full pattern at the top. The number two strip will have a half-pattern at the top; the number three strip will also have the full pattern at the top. The drop-match pattern gives your room a less repetitious, more varied look, which is often desired.

Every once in a long while you may come across a quarter-drop pattern. The match points on this paper come together so that when you start with a full pattern at the top of your first sheet, the second sheet will only have a quarter of the pattern at the top; the third sheet will have one half the pattern, and the fourth sheet will have three-quarters of the pattern. The fifth sheet will again have a full pattern.

POINTERS ON LINING UP THE STRAIGHT PATTERN

First make certain the pattern is designed right. If it's properly designed it will fit together on a horizontal line; otherwise you will be in trouble. Check ahead of time by doubling the paper at a match point. Notice if the crease is at the same spot in the matching element when you have lightly creased the paper. If not, you should decide whether or not you want to trim the pattern to correct the defect, or if you want a refund or exchange.

Trimming

Check alignment of edges before hanging; compare edges for alignment while wet. Take the full width of a strip of paper by about 10 to 12 inches long; paste it and then cut it down the center. Put the left half to the right of the original right half, which lets you line up the match points just as if you were matching up two strips of wallpaper. Notice if the match points line up perfectly.

Take a second strip of the same size, but strip $1/32$ inch off each edge. Then do the same as with the first test strip, trying to match up the retrimmed edges.

Compare the pretrimmed and the self-trimmed match and see if the second is an improvement. If so, you have to do some trimming. If you have to retrim, you will almost certainly have a noticeable seam that comes to a good match, but this should be better than a pattern out of alignment. Trimming requires a straightedge and a sharp knife.

CUTTING WALL COVERING

Roll the wall covering out on the paste table (or whatever cutting board you are using) and locate the point at which you want the pattern to begin on the wall. This point will meet the ceiling edge. You will be looking for the point at which a full pattern begins. Make sure the top of the material is to your left, always. From the point selected as the top of the first strip, measure the height of the wall (down to the top of the baseboard), and add one to two inches extra at the top, and the same at the bottom. Use a straightedge at right angles and cut the strip off with a razor blade.

All wall covering strips, whether they reach from the ceiling to the baseboard, the baseboard to the edge of a window, or from the ceiling to the top of a door casing, should run about four to six inches longer than the area being papered. This allows two to three inches of overlap at the top, and the same amount at the bottom. Because some wall coverings are patterned with a drop-match design, the strips often have more than the suggested four-to-six-inches. If so, cut off the additional excess, or it will interfere with hanging.

Before cutting the second strip note the amount of excess above the first strip, and if more than a few inches, remove extra material. After cutting your second in the same manner, match the third strip to the second, the fourth to the third, etc. Usually four strips at a time is enough to handle. Keep them arranged in the order they were cut.

LINING UP THE DROP MATCH PATTERN

Repeat the process described for lining up a straight-pattern wall covering. Then check to see if the match points on the right side and left side of the paper are the same at the tops and bottoms of the strips. If they are, you can take a simple step to save paper: use strips from separate rolls for alternate strips. Thus, you can hang your first strip from one roll, and use a second roll for the strip on the right. This saves paper because you don't have to worry about trimming paper from the original roll in order to reach the right match point for the top of the next strip.

If you're going to use strips from alternate rolls, it's a good idea to mark the rolls lightly with a pencil so you won't mix up the strips.

LINING UP THE QUARTER-DROP PATTERN

These are so complicated that the best procedure is to use four rolls, one for each numbered strip in the sequence. Match the join-points so the second, third, and fourth strips in a sequence add more to the pattern as you go to succeeding strips.

PASTING AND FOLDING

Unless you're hanging a prepasted wall covering, you should observe a few steps in applying paste to the wall-side of the strips you'll be hanging. By now, you should have several properly cut strips ready for application. They should be laid on the table, face down in a stack.

Put the top ends of the sheets to the left of the table, making certain you have a smooth surface on which to apply paste.

Load the seven-inch paint roller, with its ⅜ inch nap, from the paste bucket—just enough so it won't drip—then draw it down the middle of the strip, starting about 2 inches from the top end so you can leave the area to be trimmed off unpasted. Continue halfway down the table. Work the paste on this strip toward both edges. By working out from the center you can get a smooth coat and avoid smearing the front of the paper near the edges. Never use too much paste. The roller is helpful because it deposits a more even coat of adhesive than does a brush. Repeat this step for the bottom half of the strip.

Put down the roller and with your right hand take the bottom edge of the strip and fold over so that edge will end up a bit short of the center of the strip. You now have a section of the pattern face up. Be careful not to crease at the fold.

Then take the left edge and draw it over so it will end up just beyond the edge of the bottom half. (Because you started applying adhesive about two inches from the top end, there is no adhesive to smear up the face the top edge overlaps.) Bear this in mind: ALWAYS HAVE PASTED SIDE AGAINST PASTED SIDE IN A FOLD. NEVER ALLOW PASTED SIDE TO FOLD OVER THE FACE OF THE WALL COVERING. Because the area to be trimmed off has not been pasted you grasp the entire folded section without smearing the face. This folding method allows you to conveniently carry the pasted strip from the table to the wall.

Precaution: Be certain the edges of the folds are aligned. Simply put an open hand, palm down, on the middle of the top fold and gently work the fold from side to side until the edges are lined up. Watch out for creasing and for trapped air, which can cause bubbles and a bumpy hanging job.

When selvage, or surplus margin, is present, remove with a sharp blade along a carefully placed straightedge.

Side edges of folded wall covering are lined up, ready for trimming.

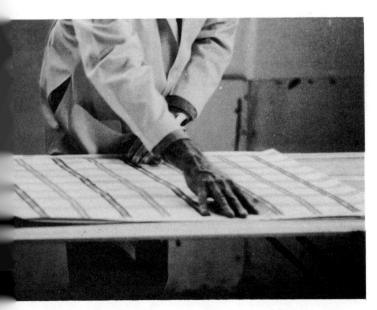

After pasting smoothly, fold edge so it ends up just short of center of strip, pattern up. Fold other edge to just beyond the edge of other fold, which should have a few inches without adhesive. Do not crease folds.

At this point, you can cut the waste edge on the sides of the strips, known as selvage, if the wall covering has any. Trim the selvage using a single-edge razor blade, or a sharp cutting tool with a handle.

Remember that paper swells, so when you cut already-pasted paper take this into account. The rate of absorption depends on the time the paper has had paste on it. Remember, too, that one end was pasted before the other, so wait until both ends have had time to swell uniformly before cutting selvage; otherwise, edge alignment will be poor.

If you decide to cut the selvage edges, then be certain to measure the amount you are to cut off from straight lines you have marked along the outer edges.

Start at the extreme right of the strip and with a straightedge carefully but not heavily run the razor blade over the line to be cut. Cut straight down. Avoid cutting on an angle because that will interfere with the joining at the seam. Always remove trim marks, which invariably are on the selvage. They are usually identified by "trim."

Not all wall coverings are trimmed after they have been pasted or folded. Metallic foils are usually put onto a pasted wall, so they are trimmed while dry. Sculptured papers have too much coating to be folded and must be trimmed differently, as we shall see. And some delicate wall coverings would crack if folded. They will be discussed later.

PREPASTED WALL COVERING

Nowadays, the selection of prepasted wall covering has so expanded that their use has become quite common. Usually, manufacturers give far better instructions for prepasted than for any other wall coverings. If instructions are not included in the wall-covering package, check the book you ordered from. Here are recommended procedures:

1. Follow the advice in the earlier sections of this chapter on wall preparation, pattern matching, and measuring.
2. Set up an inexpensive water tray; you can buy one from your wall-covering dealer. Fill it, and put it on a towel or drop cloth on the floor just below the section of the wall where the first strip is to be hung.
3. Reroll the strip you're going to put up, with the pattern-side in and with the top exposed so you will pull it out first. Place in the water tray.
4. With ladder ready, let the strip stay submerged as long as the manufacturer recommends. Then pull it out slowly, climb the ladder and apply.
5. Or you can put the water tray on a table and place the rolled strip in it as indicated in (c) on page 115. Instead

putting it on the wall directly from the tray, remove the strip slowly and put the pattern side down on a table; fold the right side over the center, with paste-side to paste-side; do the same with the left side, with no overlap at all. This is called "booking" and allows you to carry the strip to the wall without smearing the pattern-side. Or you can take the strip and lay it on a table and apply water directly to it with a brush; then book it.

6. For prepasted flocks, change water in water box often because adhesive accumulates and stiffens flocks.
7. PRECAUTION: If you apply paste to prepasted wall covering, use only very thin cellulose adhesive. Apply with brush or roller. Let it soak twice the time recommended for ordinary use.

    You are most likely to need supplementary adhesive for ceilings or over sanded walls or other rough surfaces. Wash ceilings and woodwork well, because adhesives on prepasted materials will cause stains.

Wall Markings

    To make sure the first strip is a perfect vertical, use a plumb line, which is a cord with a weight on the end. Stick a pin or tack in the wall and drop the cord, making sure that the weight falls free. You can then chalk in the line on the wall so you'll have a straight line for putting up the first strip. Drawing a horizontal line about 10 inches below the ceiling, and exactly parallel to it, also helps alignment.

c. Fill water tray. Hold bottom edge, roll up the strip, pasted side out. Weight the strip with table knife inside, submerge in the water.

d. Pattern side down, pull slowly from water. Fold as shown, paste-to-paste. Set aside to soak at least 5 minutes if wall covering is strippable. If not strippable, hang immediately after folding. Prepare second strip.

a. From left to right: One strip (less ½ inch) to the right of the door, fasten plumb line from ceiling. Chalk the string and, holding it near the bottom, snap a line onto the wall.

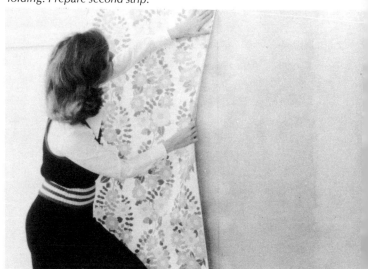

e. Unfold top part of strip only. Position near ceiling, leaving 3 inches to trim later. Line up the right edge of the strip with the plumb line.

b. Measure ceiling height. Allow 3 inches extra top, 3 inches at bottom. Cut one strip. Match pattern, cut two more, hang before cutting more.

f. Wet with sponge, smooth strip, working from center to edges. Unfold bottom, align with plumb line, smooth. Small bubbles disappear with drying.

g. Use ruler with knife or razor blade to trim top, bottom and around door frame. Wipe off paste with wet sponge. Sponge entire strip. Roll down edges with a seam roller. Don't use roller on flock wall coverings. Tap seams with sponge to avoid matting flock pile.

h. Dip and hang succeeding strips. Carefully match pattern at left edge of new strip with previous strip. Butt edges, sponge, and roll edges.

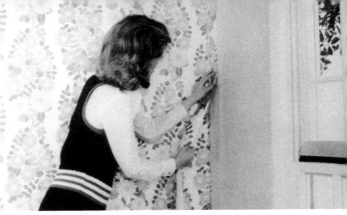

i. Measure edge-to-corner at top, middle and baseboard. Take widest measure. Add ½ inch. Cut vertical strip this width. Apply, overlap corner. Measure remainder of strip. Add ½ inch. Drop plumb this distance from corner. Follow plumb, apply, match and lap at corner.

j. Measure to frame. Add 1 inch. Cut vertical strip to this width. Apply so it extends over top of frame 1 inch. Trim around frame. Match pattern; use short lengths above, below frame.

k. Alternate method. Use drop cloth. Place water box at baseboard. Slowly unroll thoroughly wet strip. Align with plumb line. Follow steps 6 through 10. (Photos: Imperial Wallcoverings, A Collins & Aikman Co.).

Hanging—
The Final Steps

MACHINE-PRINTED WALLPAPERS

Untrimmed Machine-Printed Wallpapers

As a rule, simply paste and fold the wallpaper, as indicated earlier. Then trim and hang—unless the paper has to have time to absorb the paste, or "soak" in it. If so, set aside the first strip after coating it with paste. Then paste and fold a second strip and lay it aside to soak without trimming it.

You will know that you need to soak the paper if it does not seem to soften appreciably when paste is put on. That means moisture has not been absorbed and the wall may absorb too much moisture, leaving insufficient adhesive on the paper for it to stick. Let paste soak until you can see the paper has become soft and flexible.

Hang the first strip and then take the second, still-soaking strip, and trim it. Paste and fold a third strip without trimming it; take the trimmed second strip and hang it. Repeat the procedure for succeeding strips.

Roll up the soaking strips and arrange them so you will know which went in first. Put them in a large plastic garbage bag. The humid condition will speed up soaking.

When you have applied each strip, run a moderately wet sponge over the new seam to remove any dried paste that may have oozed out. Then, with clean water and a sponge, wash the seam.

Pretrimmed Machine Prints

Because these have no blank edges, or selvage, the ready-trimmed edges may dry out. You may have to allow more time for soaking; the plastic bag treatment will be especially helpful.

Because sometime the factory doesn't do a good trimming job it may be necessary to check alignment of opposite edges and trim as described on page 113.

After hanging, wash each seam as described for untrimmed wallpaper.

High humidity inside closed plastic garbage bag speeds soaking of stiffer materials.

Prepasted Wallpapers

Prepasted wallpapers are easiest to hang on porous and moderately porous walls because the heavy paste will be sucked into them. Hard, impermeable surfaces such as those with glossy or semi-gloss paints, will not draw in this paste and an excess will build up between paper and wall. Avoid this by wetting several sheets ahead before applying them, and letting the adhesive firm up by partial drying so that running won't occur.

Many of the problems formerly caused by hard surfaces have been overcome by use of an emulsion bonding agent or size over the hard surface.

To avoid air bubbles under paper on these hard or sealed surfaces, some paperhangers find it helpful to smooth out the heavy paste under the paper by running a flat smoothing device over the paper. Again, clean seams after hanging.

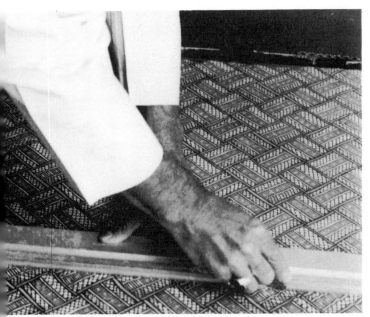

When stiffness is a problem on irregular surfaces, leave selvages on first and second strips and line them up on wall. Cut through both selvages and you have double-cut perfect seams.

Strippable Wallpapers

Strippable wallpapers consist of paper reinforced with up to 20 percent of synthetic fibres. Because these papers have been treated for easy removal without the use of water or other aids, they feel differently from other wallpaper.

Most strippable papers are somewhat stiff. One type, Tyvek, will not absorb moisture. All types have the advantage of breathing, which means no mildew, and can be hung with wheat paste or cellulose. They are also washable and almost tearproof. Tyvek material can be pasted directly, or the paste can go on the wall.

The less stiff types are easier to hang, but will tear. Some are washable. They must be pasted directly.

Stiff papers sometimes do not meet exactly even when the papers have been printed accurately and have straight edges. Because they are stiff, they do not readily accommodate irregularities in the surface being covered.

Professionals try to overcome this by "double cutting." This sounds tougher than it is. You leave the selvage on the first and second strips. Line the selvage of the second strip up with that of the first, putting it directly on top. Keep sliding the entire second strip over until the second-strip selvage, on top, is completely past the bottom selvage. You now have the two selvages side by side. The bottom selvage on the first strip has been covered by the pattern.

Now, when you cut with enough pressure you can peel off the top selvage. Lift up the top strip edge that covers the bottom strip selvage and remove the bottom selvage. Replace the top strip and you have a perfect seam. Don't cut too hard, or you will damage the wall. Since the paste is still wet, you can adjust the paper if necessary.

Soaking and Growing. It is best to know before beginning application whether or not the strippable wallpaper can be hanged immediately after being pasted. To find out, take a small waste piece and apply paste. If it is not flexible right away, then about 10 minutes later check again. It will need soaking for whatever time required for it to become soft, probably the full 10 minutes used for the test, maybe less if you notice it has softened faster.

Some papers "grow" upon soaking—sometimes as much as one half inch. They do not shrink back. When your test strip indicates the paper will grow, allow a long soaking period in a plastic bag to ensure even stretching of all the strips.

Prepasted. Sometimes prepasted strippable papers cause problems because the adhesive gets too tacky too soon. This makes it difficult to slip the paper over into the proper seam position. The best way to get around it is to sponge up the section of the wall at about the point where the center of the strip will go. Then slide the paper over this, borrowing fluidity from the wet area.

HAND-PRINTED WALLPAPERS

Hand-Screened Prints on Flat Paper Stock

These medium-weight papers form seams that may be almost invisible if done with care. Because the low-sheen finish absorbs moisture, these papers require only brief soaking unless they are printed with heavy oil colors. If so, soaking must follow a few simple rules.

With heavy-oil inks, the paper around the pattern will absorb more adhesive than the paper bearing the pattern. Naturally, the amount of swelling will vary as a result. This causes wrinkling, especially if you try to hurry. So let the adhesive soak a while longer, using the plastic bag as a means of speeding the soak period. Any wrinkles left after soaking will smooth out if a soft brush, cloth or roller is drawn across the strip after it is hung, before it dries.

All of these flat paper strips should be gently rolled after they have had a chance to set a while, but before they have dried completely. Hang two or three strips and then go back and put gentle pressure on the first seam that was formed. Repeat this after each strip is laid; come back and gently roll the next seam in sequence.

Hand-Screened Prints on Calendar or Glossy Paper

These papers are fast disappearing. Their major drawback is curling at the seams, which means it is hard to paste and fold them. You can cope with this by sponging the back of the strip, all over, with tap water before applying the paste. The strip will lie flat when enough water has been absorbed. Then apply an even coat of thick paste, but not heavily. Fold, trim and apply as usual. Be certain to immediately wash off any paste that reaches the surface.

Since glossy papers highlight surface defects, you must have a smooth surface. For this reason, professionals prefer using lining paper. This also holds the seams together; otherwise, they tend to pull up as they dry.

Hand-Screened Flock Papers

Flocks with their soft, somewhat velvety surfaces, provide interesting effects on the wall. Patterns can utilize the effect of light on the transparent material, regarded by some as luxurious.

Flock papers present several problems. The plastic particles—or flock—often fall off in manufacture or shipment, and dust may rise when you open the roll. A wet handkerchief over the nose when working with these

Safeguard flock facing when irregular surface requires double-cutting by using wax paper, kitchen plastic, or masking tape over the bottom flock. This will protect it from adhesive on the top strip.

should provide ample protection, but if the job is large a dust mask may be advisable.

Another problem involves seaming the flock papers. If the seams are pressed too hard, the flock around the seam may flatten and look different. The seam will stand out, which it should not.

If you have a flock paper that flattens even with modest pressure, try to fluff it up with a small brush or a firm sponge. Check the sponge in an inconspicuous area to see if it mars the flock.

Sometimes satisfactory seams have been achieved by pressing on the edges with the tips of a smoothing brush rather than pressing with a roller. The tips affect fewer flock particles.

It is important to avoid surplus paste in hanging flocks, so lining paper is often necessary. Even with lining paper, it is essential that an even coat of adhesive is applied to prevent oozing at the seams. Paste is hard to remove from flock, and if it runs in a long line at the seam it can be clearly identified. Medium-thick paste is best.

To prevent oozing, try coating the area where you know the seam will fall with a four-inch-wide line of adhesive. Draw a knife or some straight device over the coating, leaving a thin coat that should dry rather quickly. This tacky wall area will grip the edges of the flock paper and cause it to lie flat without oozing. This will also keep flock paper from curling at the edge.

If you find it necessary to double-cut, remember that flock will come off on the glue-coated area. Put a sheet of wax paper or kitchen plastic between strips to protect the under strip from the glue. Be certain to remove the wax paper before completing the seam.

Hand-Screened Textured Wallpapers

These are actually three-dimensional wall coverings with a rather thick buildup of ground cork base and oil paint. They require careful attention to prevent cracking.

There are two kinds: one comes on white paper, and is less difficult to hang; the other comes on brown paper. The white paper version should be coated and allowed to soak with medium-thick wheat paste until it becomes flexible.

Until satisfactory cellulose adhesives were developed, lining was necessary for hanging these materials. Even now you should check adhesion by hanging a sample strip overnight.

Watch out for the following trouble spots.

1. Trim the sheet particularly well to avoid much adjusting, since the thick buildup of ground cork and paint makes it susceptible to cracking with movement.
2. Make very loose folds to avoid cracking.
3. Roll seam edges very gently so the cork and paint won't wear away and expose the paper.
4. Where overlaps occur at corners or arches, remove the cork granules on the understrip so they won't bulge out on the overlap. Use fine sandpaper.
5. Where these brittle papers come up against ceilings, door, or window moldings, be extra careful. Roll the paper against the encountered surface with a small corner roller, and then trim.

Remember, you can touch up small breaks in the painted area with a flat paint of a suitable color.

Textured wall coverings on brown paper, more difficult to hang than the white, must be dry-trimmed. A medium thick vinyl adhesive is best. Strips should be coated evenly. Coat three or four and put in a plastic lawn bag to soak. After removing each soaked strip, paste it evenly again and then hang.

VINYL WALL COVERINGS

The term "vinyl" covers a multitude of materials of varying quality. It is best to understand what a true vinyl is before buying products that may or not be actual vinyls.

A vinyl wall covering is made in part of a plastic ma-terial whose name is polyvinyl chloride; because this is a very hard plastic it is usually combined with a softer vinyl chemical such as polyvinyl acetate. The resulting chemical is made into a sheet, printed, and then cut into rolls for wall covering sales rooms.

Other so-called vinylized or vinyl-coated materials are usually paper with a coat of a clear plastic—often a member of the vinyl family—sprayed or rolled over them to make them easier to clean, or water-repellent.

True vinyls are now the most popular wall covering because of the wide pattern selection, and because they are strong and easy to remove.

It is no harder to hang vinyls than any other wall covering. They are different, but not necessarily difficult. You must simply keep several points in mind. Vinyls are nonbreathing, which means that moisture in the paste applied cannot escape through the surface as it does with paper. There is a tendency, partly because of its non-breathability, to develop air pockets unless you carefully smooth out the surface.

Paste selection is important, and you must take into account its moisture content and the porousness of the wall. Weight of the vinyl and its backing—paper or cloth—also determine to a great extent adhesive selection.

Paperbacked Vinyls

These vinyls are available in both pretrimmed, machine-printed, and hand-printed. Pretrimmed, machine-printed vinyls offer few problems. Hand-printed, paper-backed vinyls, however, have edges required by the silk-screen process. These edges often cut somewhat unsatisfactorily at the folds, and the professional method is to keep the folded material lined up as well as possible while cutting, but to stop cutting about three or four inches before reaching the curve of the fold, which is where an unsatisfactory match is likely to show up.

At the point where you stopped cutting, reverse the cutting direction and trim from the curve of the fold on into the uncut portion until you reach the point at which you stopped. Watch carefully that you cut evenly from the edge of the selvage, which is the unusable edge.

Here are the steps for hanging paper-backed vinyls:

1. Make certain you apply an even coat of adhesive, using a short-nap roller.
2. Hang your first strip so that it is certain to go beyond one of the corners by a small distance. Keep it straight by using a plumb line. Having a straight line on each side of the corner assures you of two straight guidelines.
3. When hanging second strip, line up the seam on the top portion of the strip first, without pressing the strips so hard that entrapped air cannot be removed
4. When the adhesive has set enough to hold the strips,

use the smoothing device to put modest pressure on the top portion of the seam.

5. Now, use the smoother to work out any entrapped air bubbles—moving toward the far edge—not toward the seam. Start at the bottom of the section already pasted down (remember, the bottom portion is still loose) and then work up to the top, smoothing at right angles to the seam.

6. See if the seam is still properly butted and then roll it with a little more pressure than before.

7. After you have trimmed the top half and cleaned whatever needs cleaning, do the same with the bottom half.

8. Professionals use two lights when hanging vinyls; so should you. A strong light directly on the wall will help you to see if the seam is correctly butted; a side light, right or left, will reveal trapped air bubbles or too much adhesive. Shut off the back light after every three or four strips, and examine your work with the side light.

You may find some of the troubles described previously: seams may curl on some heavier stocks; the strips may not slip on because of tacky adhesive. If so, use the methods given earlier.

Cloth-backed Vinyls

Vinyls with gauze or fabric laminated to them are tear-resistant and strippable. Consequently, you can easily repair lifted seams and, when you want to remove the vinyls, you simply pull off and wash off the old adhesive. You can then apply new wall covering or paint.

Cloth-backed vinyls are less likely than the paper-backed to be affected by temperature and moisture, so bonds and seams are usually intact throughout all seasons.

Vinyls with cloth backing range from thin and flexible to heavy and stiff. Thin vinyls often call for vinylized wheat paste, which can cause shrinking of the cloth backing without adequate soaking. But because some backing will delaminate, soaking should be kept to a minimum. Soaking time should be the same for all strips for uniform shrinkage.

Heavyweight Vinyls

Both professional craftsmen and homeowners formerly were reluctant to use these heavy materials because of the sheer difficulty of getting them on the wall. Today, with a few exceptions, the heavier materials have disappeared from the market and lighter materials have taken their place without sacrifice of durability.

Because heavy vinyls come in 54-inch widths, many craftsmen prefer using two box tables in order to have enough working room. Still others prefer working on the floor. For big jobs, craftsmen can now rent or buy

Use the smoother to work out entrapped bubbles; work toward far edge, not existing seam.

patented pasting machines, which handle the job easily and quickly.

For these wide, heavy materials, a premixed adhesive must always be used—in most cases applied to the material. In some instances it has been found advantageous to paste the wall.

The heavier materials must be double-cut to assure satisfactory seams. Use a straightedge held firmly, and a sharp razor blade. To be certain you do not cut the wall, put a strip of foil or light vinyl beneath the wall covering.

Vinyl Suedes

These new materials resemble the elegant material used in sport coats. Some of the most popular fabrics are imported from Belgium.

Since these products have a pile, like suede or velvet, the strips all must be hung going in the same direction. Our experience has shown best results when pasting the wall and hanging dry strips.

Keeping adhesive off the face. Hang the first sheet at least six inches away from a corner, to allow plenty of room for double-cutting and for wrapping the next sheet around the corner.

On top of the first sheet paste a 2-inch strip of masking tape to the strip edge (this edge will be trimmed later, so the adhesive on the masking tape does not matter). Put adhesive over this tape when pasting the wall for the adjoining strip. When you apply the next strip align it to the edge of the tape so that the second strip covers the tape.

Mylar has several advantages, such as washability, good printability, excellent seaming, outstanding strength, and easy overlapping.

However, installation must be done with great care because the material is easily scratched. Adhesive should be kept off the face, because a haze may remain.

In installation, Mylar resembles foil because it is trimmed dry, and the wall is pasted rather than the material. Since Mylar is a nonbreather, a vinyl adhesive should be used. A moist adhesive is desirable, to soften and relax the sheet. If the adhesive used is not moist enough, then wet the back of the material before putting it on the wall.

If adhesive gets on the face, use Windex or a similar, ammonia-based cleaner to avoid haze.

FOIL WALL COVERING

Aside from some not-too-severe problems in trimming, foils are little more difficult to hang than wallpaper. They're actually less difficult than most of the vinyls.

You must remember that foils are really aluminum foil—roughly the same grade used for kitchen wrap, but laminated to either paper or cloth. While the foil itself won't absorb water, the backing will.

Paper-backed Foil

The paper backing may cause curling during application, and the combination of foil and paper backing may cause a humping effect on the trimming table; put extra weight on the edge of the strip not yet trimmed so the roll as a whole will not hump. Otherwise, you may find you've trimmed one-eighth inch from the top and bottom edges, leaving a wide middle area. This will ruin the butting of adjacent strips.

To avoid this, try to cut your strips only five or six feet long. When trimming one side, make certain the entire strip lies flat; use a long board or a long straightedge to hold the opposite edge just as flat as the side you're trimming. Before trimming, make certain that the right edge widths are the same at top, bottom—and MIDDLE. Then trim.

If you must cut strips longer than six feet, do the same thing but use a shorter straightedge, about three feet, and only trim three feet at a time, checking edges to assure a true measure all the way down on both sides.

Trouble with curling of paper-backed foil can be cured by lining the wall with 10-ounce lining paper, and then pasting this rather than the wall covering.

The lining paper will soak up the excess moisture and when you put up the dry-trimmed foil wall covering, its paper back is not likely to absorb enough moisture to cause curling.

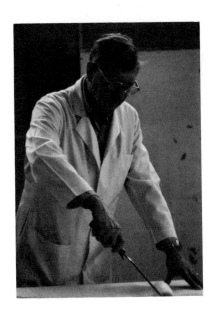

For application of Mylar polyester, use a moist adhesive to soften and relax the strip.

Double-cut at its edge, along the edge of the second strip and masking tape underneath. Lift the new edge and remove the material underneath (the edge of the first piece and the masking tape that tops it).

Be extra careful about keeping the premixed adhesive off the face of the suede, because the paste leaves a haze when removed. A chemical remover minimizes the haze, but does not completely control it. Another precaution: when overlapping vinyl materials, a special vinyl-to-vinyl material must be used. After completing the overlaps (usually at dormers, arches, and wall-to-ceiling junctures), apply heat with a hair dryer to soften the material and to help the adhesive hold more firmly.

Mylar (Polyester)

Rapidly growing in importance, Mylar is not a vinyl. Because it is a synthetic material it is included here.

You will want to cut and trim about four strips ahead of time so you can match them. If you have random patterns and matching is not involved, you may want to reverse alternate strips to get more interesting light effects. Number the backs of the strips so you'll know the sequence.

When you roll up these individual strips, make sure that the top of the sheet is on the outside of the roll.

Now you're ready to hang.

1. Mark a plumb line for the first strip.
2. Use a narrow brush, about 2 inches, to apply paste where your paste roller can't reach, then roll paste over the areas to be covered by the first strip, going two inches over the plumb line.
3. Apply the first strip with the edge lined up against the plumb line.
4. Take your smoothing brush and run it straight down the middle of the strip, starting at the top. Then, from the top in the middle, work all the way down. Move horizontally from the middle to each side. This way you smooth the foil and eliminate air bubbles.
5. Gently roll the foil edge so that it will not smear the next sheet.

Repeat the process for the next strip. To prevent paste from reaching the first strip, take a one-inch strip of some cloth-backed selvage or other remnant, and paste it up next to the first strip. Let it get tacky enough so that it won't ooze adhesive onto the first foil strip, but not so tacky that it won't stay wet when you remove it a few minutes later.

Now that you've put this strip where the seam will be, paste the lined wall just as you did for the first strip. Then lift up the one-inch strip. Adhesive will be there just as elsewhere on the lined wall area, just up to the first strip but without danger of paste going onto it. Now hang the second strip in the same manner as the first. After you have followed the procedure for smoothing down the paper from top to bottom, roll the seam so it will lie flat. Trim top and bottom and clean up any excess paste.

Cloth-backed Foils

Use of cloth backing for foils will soon end. Spun polyester backing is replacing cloth on foil. Spun-polyester and cloth backing both require vinyl adhesive.

If a particularly burdensome amount of rolling and smoothing is required to apply these foils, try a stronger adhesive, such as a combination of premixed vinyl and powdered vinyl.

To guard against mildew formation behind the wall covering, add two tablespoons of Lysol to each pail of paste. However, if you've prepared the walls properly, this should not be necessary.

Handle adhesive in a special way at foil seams. Use a strip of surplus remnant on wall to transfer tacky adhesive to area where foil's edge will be, and no liquid will reach face.

Special Foils

Some foils have transparent vinyl coatings. All over-lapping here requires a vinyl-to-vinyl adhesive, which is the descriptive name for a special adhesive made to join two vinyl surfaces.

Flock foils should be handled like regular foils, with the same measures depending on the backing used.

BURLAP WALL COVERINGS

Working with burlap poses no great problem as long as you remember that this rough material, formerly used for bagging cheap bulky commodities, will require special care in matching adjacent strips. You must also guard carefully against snags at seams and at the tops and bottom of strips.

Square off the ceiling edge. Check carefully for defects. You may be able to salvage the good portions that are too short for a full strip. These may be used above or below windows, arches, or doors. To aid in matching this inconsistent material, cut as many strips as is required for room—at one time—and then lay them on a flat surface to match them as closely as possible. Number the strips in the order they will be hung.

Paper-backed Burlap

Since burlap is highly absorbent, and since it usually has a paper backing, be especially careful to keep out moisture. Use far less water than usual with your adhesive, which preferably should be a powdered vinyl. Use about a half-pint less water for each six-ounce package than called for in the directions. Keep the adhesive tacky.

Burlap needs a considerable amount of this tacky adhesive to hold it to the wall. To assure this, put down a coat of adhesive with a short nap roller. This acts as a size and dries quickly. It evidently seals the paper backing and allows the second coat you will then apply to remain tacky. Hang the first strip, following earlier steps for plumbness.

To assure snag-free edges, use an especially sharp razor blade to trim an inch off each edge. Check blades frequently for sharpness, because a dull blade can cause snags. Later, when you smooth the strips down on the wall, work from the center. Stop short of the edges and use a roller only for pressing them down. This prevents damage to the edges.

Since you're dealing with a heavy material, put the second strip up so the strip edges are fairly close. Thus you won't risk having the strip slip down as you gently edge the top of the second strip toward the first. Begin by pressing down the material about two feet from the ceiling edge. Butt the edges very carefully, so the edge-fibers won't push against each other and lift.

Take extra precautions in trimming tops and bottoms. When cutting across this way, you can avoid loose threads by stopping just short of the edge. Then turn and cut the other direction, starting from the edge and cutting toward the point where you stopped.

You may find that because burlap on paper is so flexible, one side will stretch as you go around a corner, and the edge on that side may be crooked. Simply cut it straight.

While, as we observed, it is preferable to hang paper-backed burlap on a lined wall, you can put it directly on an unlined wall if you have a really good surface, smooth and free of potentially peeling paint. Be certain to use the wax paper method described previously wherever there is danger of seeping paste.

Printed Burlap

This is hung the same way as paper-backed burlap, but because it is printed you may not need to match shades quite so carefully as with ordinary burlap.

Vinylized Burlap

If you want to hang these heavy-duty, heavyweight burlaps (usually found in hospitals or institutions), then be prepared for an exacting task, but not one beyond your capability.

The required extra care is to assure that moisture does not get between the vinyl surface and the burlap. If the vinyl lifts because of moisture, the entire job can be ruined. Moisture can reach the edges from backing or from paste on adjoining strips.

Rather than pasting the seams, leave them dry and paste the wall, preferably lined, where seams will fall. After pasting, run a wide knife over the adhesive on the wall to reduce its thickness and moisture. The later pressure on the strip and the adhesive, during application, will cause it to stick.

Materials You May Want to Let a Pro Hang

Tricky wall coverings, unfortunately, are also among the most expensive you're likely to encounter. If you're really careful and meticulous; if you have a lot of self-confidence; if you are dexterous and really like to prove to yourself that you can respond successfully to a sporting challenge, then you can probably hang these difficult wall coverings.

But close attention to instructions is essential—all the way.

Even if you decide to let a professional mechanic hang these wall coverings, read this section so you can keep an eye on what's being done and will know if your expensive fabrics or silks are in danger of ruin.

Included in this category of difficult but not impossible materials are textile fabrics, including cotton, linen and silk, felt, and grass cloth.

LIGHT TEXTILE FABRICS

Fine light silk, linen, and cotton fabrics without backing expand the range of truly delicate and sensitive designs for the discriminating homeowner with the wherewithal to buy them.

Upon buying them, no matter who does the hanging, make absolutely certain that the material is preshrunk. Otherwise, you're in for trouble.

If no guarantee is given, test the fabric yourself by cutting out a square foot or so as a sample and putting it on the wall; mark around it to show its original size. Then paste it on the wall, using the recommended adhesive (usually a powdered vinyl), taking care that you apply it within the marked off space.

Leave it on the wall for 30 to 45 minutes and see if there is a gap between the fabric and the original outline. If so, it's not preshrunk. But don't give up just because it shrinks. Make a few more tests: adjust the paste's moisture content, check various levels until you find a combination that reduces shrinkage to a manageable level.

Another check: how well will the fabric shed any adhesive that may land on its face? Find out by spotting up a sample. Sponge off a few spots immediately, and see if the remaining moisture from the spongeing can be removed. Let some of the paste spots dry and see if they can be removed.

Once you decide the fabric can be used, you must put lining paper on the wall. Follow steps given in earlier chapters.

Cut your strips, leaving square edges at the top. Trim one of the edges, removing selvage, if any. If no selvage is present, you will probably have to cut off as much as necessary to match up with the edge of the next strip. So that cut edges are not frayed or frazzled, press hard on your straightedge while cutting, and use sharp cutting edges.

You will want to use two plumb lines for the first strip, so you will have straight markings to aim at while pulling these stretchable fabrics into position.

With the plumb lines up, apply an even film of powdered vinyl adhesive to the wall, using much less water than the directions require, about a half-pint less or whatever you need for a decidedly tacky surface. Do not use a powdered-vinyl *wheat* paste adhesive.

The fabric, which should be rolled up on a mop handle or something similar, with the face on the inside, should be brought up against the ceiling between plumb lines and held there by a second person.

Once you know the fabric placed on the top of the wall has adhered, roll the material onto the pasted wall.

Press down gently with hands from center to sides as you work down. Be careful to avoid causing folds or creases, and check to see if trapped air is left, although the fabric will later release it.

For the second strip, do not apply paste all the way to the edges of the fabric. Use narrow strips of cloth-backed material for paste-transfer, as described under "Vinyl Suedes." Then paste as you did for the first strip, using a

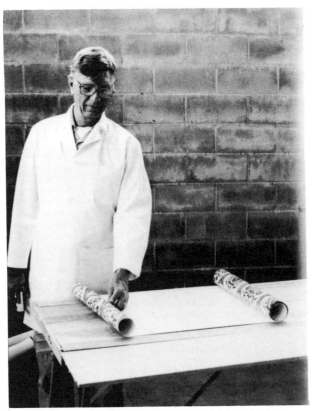

Paperback, light fabric tends to roll, so clip to edge of table when pasting. When soaked sufficiently, rolling up will stop.

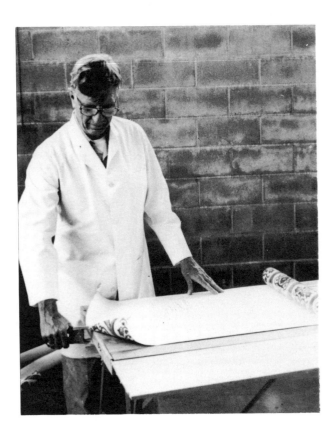

plumb line for the outer edge. When ready to apply the fabric remove the transfer strips, which will leave a tacky film of adhesive, and repeat the rolling-out procedure.

Light, Backed Materials

Paper backing, which rarely causes problems, is now used extensively for light fabric wall covering, usually on lined walls. Vinyl powdered adhesive is best.

The firmness of the backing helps eliminate the problem of the wavering look light fabrics often have on the wall, and the seepage of the paste to the face that often mars the fabric-hanging job is less likely to occur with paper backing. Paper also binds the fibres and prevents unravelling.

Hanging these paper-backed fabrics is similar to application of burlap. Set up your roll on a broomhandle, if necessary, and pull your strips off all at one time, numbering them as they will be used across the room. Be certain to include in the sequence of numbers those strips that will be cut later for windows and doors.

Double-trimming. Because the edge beyond the pattern, known as the selvage, is often uneven, you should even up both sides by a simple step known as "double-trimming." Pick some detail in the pattern of the fabric. With a straightedge, measure off a distance from the fabric to a point in the selvage; find the same detail in the same pattern lower down on the strip, and measure off the same distance. Quite clearly, the line connecting these points should be equidistant from the edge of the pattern all the way down.

To "double-trim," do the same thing on the opposite selvage. The result: a pattern with equal selvage on both sides, which makes it easy to trim. (If the selvages are straight in the first place, don't worry about this step.)

To handle the problem of edges rolling up, affix a paper clip (the type used for keeping a sheaf of papers in a clipboard) to a smooth board or some molding. Let this hold the top edge of the material.

With the edges held straight, trim as you would other materials and then paste, using powdered vinyl adhesive. Use a plumb line for hanging the first strip, and smooth out any trapped air.

The next strip should be worked down from the top, about three feet at first, leaving a tiny gap between it and the previously hung strip so you can slowly slide this strip over for a tight, but not too tight, butt. If too tight, the threads at the edges may lift.

You can tell if the adhesive is too stiff because the shifting of the strip will be difficult. If so, dilute the paste a bit for the third strip, adjusting until you get the right feel.

For a really good job, try to have a little excess length at the ceiling line. Make certain the material is rolled tight into the angle at the ceiling. When you trim the excess, start near the center and work out and stop about an inch from the edges. Then, start at the edges and complete the cut. This prevents frazzled edges.

Vinyl-Faced Fabrics

Fabrics protected by a sheet of laminated vinyl are hung somewhat as other paper-backed fabrics except that extra precautions are necessary to prevent moisture from seeping through and separating the vinyl from the fabric.

Using a premixed vinyl adhesive with low moisture is helpful. Having a lined wall to absorb moisture is also a good idea. Use no more adhesive than necessary. If you have trouble getting the seams to lie flat, prepaste the seam area but be certain that adhesive is used sparingly. Scrape off all but a minimum amount to insure that no seepage will occur.

Shiki Silk

Special techniques are required to hang this delicate oriental silk, whose light texture, if you look closely, is distinguished by horizontal bands.

Cut your strips the proper length and lay them out next to each other so you can decide how to place them. Colors and shades vary, sometimes subtly, sometimes obviously. These are natural materials, and show the best and worst in nature. This gives them a dramatic quality. Some recommend shading or matching strips as well as possible, but the most effective procedure is to apply the cloth in strips as it comes from the roll.

Since these delicate silks will almost certainly curl up, use a large clip and a board to keep the strips straightened.

Use lining paper on the walls. To apply paper-backed silk to the lining, use cellulose paste. Each strip should be pasted separately, with care to avoid excess paste on edges. Use a short-nap roller and coat as evenly as possible. You'll discover that this paste dries quickly when applied so thin. Be careful when trimming; don't apply too much weight on the straightedge because it may dry the adhesive and cause the folded silk to stick together.

You have to move quickly after trimming. Hang a plumb line, which should be marked with faint chalk so it won't show through the silk.

Don't worry about the excess silk beyond the ceiling line; trim that off later. The idea is to quickly get the strip up and tightly butted, so your adhesive won't set and the paper backing won't become so wet that the facing will be ruined.

Keep moisture off the face, since this can cause the silk to delaminate from the paper backing. Cellulose paste, in small quantities, can be removed if you gently moisten it with a cloth or sponge and then follow with a dry cloth to pick up the moisture.

Silk with Hand Prints

These offer the same problems as Shiki silk. In addition, the unprinted edges are often uneven and have to be equalized, using the double-trim method already described.

GRASS CLOTH

This wallcovering should be applied like Shiki silk—in the sequence it comes from the roll, and as nature intended.

For those who want consistent color and texture, science now offers synthetic grass cloth made of cellulose. Synthetic grass cloth has another advantage compared to natural: the paper backing is more firmly laminated than on the natural grass cloth. When pasting, carefully control the soaking time. Too long a soak will cause separation of the backing and the natural grass cloth.

Depending on whether or not you have a porous wall, you may not have to use lining paper. Try the wall by putting up a small piece of material, making certain that the paste you use is medium-thick. If the trial run shows the wall will absorb the moderate amount of moisture in this paste, you won't need lining paper.

We reminded you earlier that materials in this section require great care. Grass cloth is no exception. Try to avoid having a strip end up so near a corner or a door or window that the final strip next to any one of these will be narrow. Otherwise the whole wall may be thrown out of balance. Be sure the strips on any one wall are the same width.

This often means that you have to cut all the strips down to a size that will permit a given number of strips to be divided equally into the width of the wall. For example, if you have a wall that is 204 inches wide, and your grass cloth strips are 36 inches, then you'll find that you will need five strips, and still have 24 inches of wall to cover. (Five times 36 inches totals 180 inches.) The bare 24 inches would have to be filled by a strip trimmed down from 36 inches to 24 inches, which would throw the entire wall off balance because of pattern and shading differences.

The solution is simple: just use six strips, but first cut two inches from each of the six (six times 34 inches totals 204 inches). The formula is: go to the next higher number of strips (5 to 6, 6 to 7, etc.). Multiply that number by the width of the strips; subtract from this figure the width of the wall. The remainder should be divided by the number of strips to find out how much to trim from each strip.

You don't want to cut too much to accomplish this, because if you're using full 36-inch strips on adjoining walls, and there's too big an adjustment on the problem wall, it could look bad. You wouldn't want 28-inch strips, for example. Usually, 30 inches is as narrow as you would want.

Butting the edges of grass cloth can cause trouble because it does not stretch horizontally. You can, however, stretch it lengthwise; you'll find the troublesome edge can be brought into the right position by pulling lengthwise on the edges opposite the one that doesn't meet its neighbor. If that doesn't work, you may have to crimp up on the faulty edge, creating a wrinkle which you can usually smooth over with a plastic roller.

In working with a natural grass cloth, remember too much moisture soaking into the paper backing will cause separation. So try a little adhesive on a sample to see how medium-thick paste works and how long you can soak it. Three or four minutes should be right, but if the paper separates, cut the time.

Also, be certain to keep moisture off the face when cleaning adjacent surfaces.

Synthetic Grass Cloth

These differ from natural grass cloth in their synthetic cellulose base and their consistent shading.

Because cellulose is very absorbent, paste moisture is drawn into it very quickly and pasting and folding must be done in a hurry. Paste and fold, trimming a half-inch off each edge, and then hang before the cellulose becomes mushy.

Quite often, edges of these synthetics are not straight, so you should dry-trim the strips before you paste and then double-trim them.

FELT FABRIC

Felt wall covering provides an interesting soft surface, offering sound absorption in addition to beauty. In music rooms, or where clutter or chatter is likely, felt reduces sound volume. Felt wall covering can be bought either paper-backed or plain.

A lined wall is preferable for the paper-backed. Keep paste off the surface of the material because it is difficult to remove; never use water for removal—it will cause shrinkage. Try to remove adhesive by placing Scotch tape or masking tape on the surface, and hope it will be transferred. Try to keep adhesive from pushing out over the edges when you butt them. Pressure near the edges can force out adhesive, which will deface the felt.

As a preventive measure, cover the edge of the pasted side of the felt with a three-inch strip of thin plastic all along one edge so that the plastic will fold up over the felt edges. You can then press down on the rest of the sheet without squirting adhesive onto the adjoining sheets. After applying the plastic to both edges, fold as usual, taking care that adhesive does not touch the surface.

Arrange the first strip so it begins beyond a corner by a half inch. Allow about two inches of waste each for ceiling and ends. After hanging, trim the top and bottom excess. Paste the second sheet, again adding the plastic. Apply it, arranging the edge butt to the first sheet so that it has about two inches of overlap. This puts the plastic-protected edge of the sheet directly over that of the first sheet. You can measure in advance the first sheet's plastic strip and mark it onto the second strip so the overlap will be exact.

With the second sheet trimmed all around and with all air bubbles smoothed out, use a straightedge to double-cut the edges. You must, of course, go through the felt and the plastic strips, so cut firmly but not hard enough to cut the wall. Remove the cutout materials and you should have perfect seams, with no paste peeking through them.

For unbacked felt, paste the wall. To keep paste off the face paste a one-inch wide paperbacked vinyl strip next to the edge of the first sheet before pasting the wall for the second sheet. Paste the wall for the second sheet, except the area covered by the vinyl strip. By this time, the adhesive on the vinyl strip should have become tacky enough so that when the vinyl strip is removed, the felt edge will stick to it firmly without allowing any paste to ooze out of the edge. After removing the strip, apply the second sheet.

This method applies to normal 24-inch wide felt. Some unbacked felt comes in bolts 72-inches wide. For these, experienced mechanics use three-inch wide cloth-backed vinyl strips, which are applied to the wall where seams are to go.

Since felt will shrink back when it dries, never pull a felt sheet into a new position if you have miscalculated your seam. Move the entire strip over.

Areas with Special Hanging Problems

CEILINGS

Ceilings introduce physical problems, mostly those of endurance and agility, rather than those requiring special skills.

Patience and strong arms will go far in successfully hanging wallcoverings on ceilings.

First, one must remember that ceilings, the last "wall" that we're to discuss, should always be hung first. Second, you should always have a second person help you, even if he does no more than hold the material while you stand on a ladder or makeshift scaffold and work the material into place, and smooth it down.

Remember also that ceilings are covered across the shorter dimension of the room. Imagine how much worse it would be trying to work with strips for the longer dimension. It's tough enough working from below, no matter what the length of the strip.

First, put up a plumb line, using tacks to hold the cord. To make this and the hanging easier, try to use two ladders and put an extension plank between them to stand on. This improvised scaffold will only put you a foot or so above the floor and will mean less ladder moving.

Since you will probably be putting up a pretty long strip, almost surely longer than the usual 8-foot wall strip, you will want to fold it carefully. The ceiling strips can be folded the usual way, or in a special accordion fold that makes it even more convenient. Each section should be at least one foot long (see illustration).

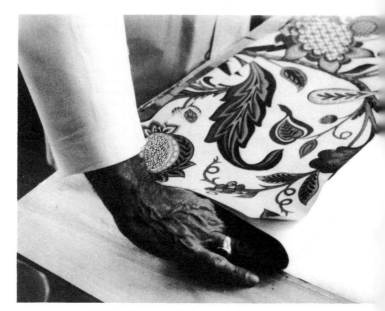

An accordian fold for the extra-long strips needed in papering ceilings: fold sections so that pasted side always faces pasted side, with each section at least 1 foot long.

Dimensions

In measuring for ceilings, be certain to allow one-half inch overlaps for all adjoining walls. That means the top and bottom of the strips need these allowances—a total of one inch for each strip—all across. Also, the two end strips need a half inch each for their *edges* to overlap onto the walls they meet.

Let's say you have a narrow dimension of 11 feet. Each strip should be at least 11 feet 1 inch long. If the

longer dimension is 19 feet, then have enough strips to cover 19 feet 1 inch, allowing one-half inch overlap for the side of the end strips.

Start hanging on the less critical side, or where it will be least noticeable.

SLANTY CORNERS

Corners that are out-of-line are an unfortunate fact of life, and everyone runs up against one (or more) sooner than later. Concede that it will lead to a mismatch, but handle it so that it will be inconspicuous.

The art of handling a mismatch is the art of playing it down. One way to do this is to wrap wall covering around the out-of-line corner so the seam to be mismatched will have as little attention drawn to it as possible.

Don't try to use the bare eye for true-ing up edges where a slant is a factor. Once the troublesome corner has been covered, and you notice the edge of the wall covering beyond the corner is at an angle, then hang the next strip to a plumb line, overlapping the angled edge. Try to take the overlap to the point that comes nearest to being a match. When trimming, do a double-cut and remove the material underneath.

WINDOWS, DOORS, AND FIREPLACES

The problem in hanging wall coverings around these wall interruptions is in keeping the pattern continuous. This is easy if you plan your job so that the strip that approaches the opening continues above the opening, leaving out that portion that would have been used if the wall had had no opening. This allows the strips above and below to meet and form matching side seams with the strips parallel to them and the opening. Again, leave an inch extension around the edges of the opening. The parts of the strip that meet the side and top moldings of the door, window, or fireplace, can be snipped at the corners and trimmed off.

Don't trust your eye in the lining up the strips above and below windows. Draw a plumb line from a point four inches below the ceiling to a point four inches below the window and mark this off so the strips below and above the window will be in line. Otherwise, you will have a real problem when hanging strips.

Since the opening will probably not be exactly the width or multiple of the width of a strip, you will have to trim the outside-edge strips above the molding so that their pattern matches the pattern of the parallel strips on the sides of the opening. After snapping and marking the plumb line at the opening, and putting up the shorter strips above and below the opening, hang the rest of the strips as you would normally. This means beginning and continuing from the corner of the room, going toward the opening where the shorter strips have already been placed. These full strips will approach the shorter ones. Measure and mark off a point where their patterns overlap exactly, so that you can double cut and have an exact match at the seams. This means that the full strips coming in from the sides will extend over the opening, and excess hanging down from these side strips will have to be trimmed off to meet the opening's molding.

DORMERS AND KNEE WALLS

Since dormers and knee walls are usually found in attics, it's a safe bet that expected slanting knee walls will be broken up by openings for windows. You will find that verticals of these window offsets adjoin angles of knee walls. While it will be possible to wrap wall covering around these tricky corners and then carefully form seams, the likelihood is trouble—unless you minimize inevitable mismatches where vertical walls leading to windows and slanting walls come together. You do this by using a pattern with considerable scattering effect, such as flowers and associated shrubbery.

Or, you can use stripes on both vertical and slanting walls. This gives an interesting zig-zag effect.

Professionals prefer to hang the routine strips—those with no special trimming—first. Then, they hang those that need to be cut on the bias and struggle with them last.

Before starting with dormers and knee walls, you may want to open your telephone book to the yellow pages and look under "paperhanger," find the most likely looking professional, and hire him.

If you don't take that advice, you may want to handle dormers by using a different material for the recessed area and the slanting knee walls. A single color, subtly patterned, or paint can be used for the vertical, and perhaps you should use a molding at the troublesome corners.

ARCHES

Plan your strip arrangement so that the strip reaching the arch has enough overlap for about two inches inside the arch itself. Cut this overlap to one-half inch. You will have to snip this one-half inch wherever necessary so it will lie down without wrinkling. If the arch is curved, rather than peaking at an angle, you will have to make several cuts in the overlap, about a half-inch apart in the curved area to help it lie wrinkle-free.

This overlap prevents fraying at the edges. It also serves a purpose if you want to apply wall covering in the arch itself. When cutting strips to decorate the inside, they should be cut just wide enough to be slightly less than the width of the arch. This allows enough room for an overlap with the first material and prevents fraying and peel-back of the inside material, which would probably occur if it went all the way to the edge.

The strips lining the vault of the arch should be applied starting from the highest point and working down. Cut them so that each side matches the other. This may cause a mismatch at the edges constituting the starting point, but that is less significant than a mismatch on the sides.

BEHIND RADIATORS

The unmistakable mark of a real amateur is loose wallpaper flapping behind a radiator.

With the paper properly pasted, simply smooth it down with a yardstick padded with cloth or rags, or a long, clean dusting brush. Since you aren't able to trim at the bottom molding, try to cut these strips reasonably accurately.

ELECTRICAL SWITCH PLATES

These, of course, are removed when wall covering is to be applied. The resulting opening should be covered with the material. Once the paste has dried, an opening not quite as large as the plate should be cut out and the plate (which has also been papered over so that the pattern is continuous) replaced.

WALL BRACKETS AND HANGING FIXTURES

Brackets and fixtures that cannot be removed cause problems. Strips that are to be hanged where these are should be marked off so that a large X-shaped cut can be made to slip over the bracket or fixture. If these are opened carefully when the wall covering is passed over the fixture, the open slits can be pasted on the wall without visibility or damage.

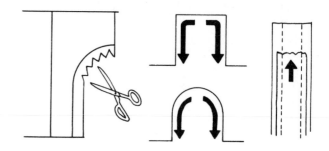

Application at arches poses special cutting problems to prevent fraying at edges. Make small cuts ½ inch apart so wall covering will wrap on the inside of the arch without wrinkling. Also, if you will be doing the top section of the arch, cut your strip so that it is long enough to start hanging from the inside top in the middle, and then continue down each side. The mismatch will not be seen underneath. Remember to leave ½ inch overlap on each side of the wall covering used underneath, ¼ inch of which goes under the covering used on the outside. Leave ¼ inch space between edge of arch and wall covering placed above overlap, to prevent fraying or peeling at overlapping edge. (Drawing courtesy of National Decorating Products Association).

DOORS, CABINETS, AND FURNITURE

Doors to rooms, closets, or cabinets can be entirely covered. A little overlap should be allowed to avoid fraying or peelback at the edges. If the adjoining walls are covered with the same material, position the paper on the door so that it will match the wall pattern.

A second way is to paint a border on the door—as wide as desired, but usually about one inch. Select a color that harmonizes with the wall covering. When this dries, hang the wall covering, after trimming it so it will be wide enough to cover about one-quarter inch of the painted border.

Cabinets other than the door portion can also be covered, as can furniture. Treat knobs, and other protuberances that can't be removed, like wall brackets. Those that can be removed should be treated like light switch covers. Edges of drawers should be treated like doors. Remember to stop before edges where fraying and rollbacks can occur.

Caution: many pieces of furniture are lacquered, which means that adhesive will not stick to them. Prime lacquered material with an emulsion-bonding agent.

MANUFACTURERS LIST

American Olean Tile Co.
Lansdale, PA 19446

American Plywood Association
1119 "A" St.
Tacoma, WA 98401

American Standard Plumbing-Heating
P.O. Box 2003
New Brunswick, NJ 08903

Astor Handprints
85 Lincoln Highway
Routes 1 & 9
South Kearny, NJ 07032

Birge Company
390 Niagara Street
Buffalo, NY 14240

California Redwood Association
617 Montgomery St.
San Francisco, CA 94111

Christopher Prints
134 Sand Park Road
Cedar Grove, NJ 07009

Columbus Coated Fabrics
1280 N. Grant Avenue
Columbus, OH 43216

Combeau Industries, Inc.
2 Decker Square
Bala Cynwyd, PA 19004

Wood Davies & Co., Ltd.
184 Front St., E.
Toronto, Ontario
Canada M5A 1E6

Jack Denst Designs, Inc.
7355 S. Exchange Ave.
Chicago, IL 60649

Eisenhart Wallcoverings Co.
P.O. Box 464
Hanover, PA 17331

Environmental Graphics
Division of Pandora Productions, Inc.
1117 Vicksburg Lane North
Wayzata, MN 55391

Formica Corp.
Formica Bldg.
120 E. 4th St.
Cincinnati, OH 45242

General Tire & Rubber Co.
401 Hackensack Avenue
Suite 704
Hackensack, NJ 07601

B.F. Goodrich General Products Co.
Division of B.F. Goodrich
500 South Main
WHB-3 D-410
Akron, OH 44318

ICI United States Inc.
Vymura Department
New Murphy Road & Concord Pike
Wilmington, DE 19897

Imperial Wallpaer Mill, Inc.
23645 Mercantile Rd.
Cleveland, OH 44122

Kohler Co.
Kohler, WI 53044

Lennon Wallpaper Co.
P.O. Box 8
Joliet, IL 60434

Lennox Wallpaper Corp.
402 W. 25th St.
N.Y., NY 10001

Lis King, Inc.
P.O. Box 603
Mahwah, NJ 07430

The Majestic Co., Inc.
Huntington, IN 46750

Malm Fireplaces, Inc.
368 Yolanda Ave.
Santa Rosa, CA 95404

Marlite, Div. Masonite
Dover, OH 44622

Masonite Corp.
29 N. Wacker Dr.
Chicago, IL 60605

Multicolor Co.
Division of National Gypsum Co.
Hatfield, MA 01038

National Decorating Products Assn.
9334 Dillman Industrial Dr.
St. Louis, MO 63132

National Forest Products Assn.
1619 Massachusetts Ave., N.W.
Washington, DC 20036

National Woodwork Manufacturers Assn.
400 W. Madison St.
Chicago, IL 60606

Saint Charles Mfg. Co.
1611 E. Main St.
St. Charles, IL

Scalamandre Wallpaper, Inc.
950 Third Ave.
N.Y., NY 10022

James Seeman Studios, Inc.
50 Rose Place
Garden City Park, NY 10040

Standard Coated Products
Formica Corporation
120 E. 4th Street
Cincinnati, OH 45202

Stauffer Chemical Co.
Westport, CT 06880

Thomas Strahan Co.
150 Heard Street
Chelsea, MA 02150

Sunworthy Division
Canadian Wallpaper Mfrs., Ltd.
222 Seventh Street
Toronto 14, Ontario, Canada

Richard E. Thibaut, Inc.
315 5th Avenue
New York, NY 10016

United-DeSoto
Wallcoverings Division of DeSoto, Inc.
3101 South Kedzie Avenue
Chicago, IL 60623

Universal-Rundle Corp.
Box 960
New Castle, PA 16103

U.S. Plywood Corp.
777 3rd Ave.
New York, NY 10017

Wall Trends International
P.O. Box 10
17 Mileed Way
Avenel, NJ 07001

Western Wood Products Association
Yeon Bldg.
Portland, OR 97204

Window Shade Manufacturers Assn.
230 Park Ave.
N.Y., NY 10017

Wood-Mode Cabinetry
Kreamer, PA 17833

York Wall Paper Company
P.O. Box 866
York, PA 17405

Z-Brick Co.
2834 N.W. Market St.
Seattle, WA 98107

INDEX